ASCENSION NOW

ASCENSION NOW
Implications of Christ's Ascension for Today's Church

Bishop Peter Atkins

A Liturgical Press Book

THE LITURGICAL PRESS
Collegeville, Minnesota

www.litpress.org

1 2 3 4 5 6 7 8 9

Library of Congress Cataloging-in-Publication Data

Atkins, Peter, 1936–
  Ascension now : implications of Christ's Ascension for today's
church / Peter Atkins.
    p. cm.
  Includes bibliographical references and index.
  ISBN 0-8146-2725-0 (alk. paper)
    1. Jesus Christ—Ascension. 2. Liturgics. I. Title.

BT500 .A75 2001
232.9'7—dc21   00-038461

Contents

Acknowledgments

The research for this book was made possible by the Board of Governors of the College of St. John the Evangelist, Auckland, New Zealand, who granted me sabbatical leave for nine months in 1996. For the first six months I was able to travel to various parts of the world to experience the variety of forms of worship on many continents and in many cultures. For the research into the doctrine of the Ascension I needed guidance from theologians and libraries that had the published literature. I was appointed to an honorary senior research fellowship at the University of Birmingham in the United Kingdom under the able supervision of Professor Frances Young and with the guidance of Dr. Gareth Jones, senior lecturer in theology. Through the kindness of Professor and Mrs. Ward at Christ Church, Oxford, we were able to live in Tom's Quad in that college. My wife, Rosemary, accompanied me throughout and gave me much inspiration and support. She has a passion equal to my own about the importance of the doctrine of the Ascension for today's Church.

I am grateful to those scholars who have looked closely into the Ascension over the years and left for us their thinking in many books. I have tried to list most of these of United Kingdom origin in the Reference Book section at the back of this volume. I acknowledge also the work of Professor Laurence Stookey of Washington in his book *Calendar: Christ's Time for the Church* (Nashville: Abingdon Press, 1996), which started my debate over the relationship between the Resurrection and the Ascension.

Finally, I acknowledge the work of the editors of The Liturgical Press for their help in bringing this text to publication. A millennium project of mine caused some delay, but I am now delighted to see the fruit of my research in print and to be added to the debates among Christians about the implications of the doctrine of the Ascension.

CHAPTER 1

Introduction:
The Importance of the Doctrine of the
Ascension for Today's Church

This book arose out of an observation that the doctrine of the Ascension of Christ has been neglected by the Church in recent years and a conviction that it is a doctrine that is vitally important to our theological debates and to the liturgical developments currently taking place in all Christian churches. Here are some of the reasons for this conviction.

In the worship of today's Church our aims are:

- to be inclusive of all who attend;
- to be sensitive to the variety of cultures we now find in the new multicultural society;
- to be true to the traditions of the Church of all the centuries;
- to meet the needs of both genders equally;
- to incorporate the gifts of both age and youth;
- to present worship and the gospel in the language best understood by those at worship;
- to relate worship to the concerns and feelings of humanity;
- to have a sense of "being with Christ" in the presence of the Trinitarian God;
- to show respect for the environment in which we live as the creation of the God whom we worship;
- to present the best of ourselves, our skills, our music, art, and architecture as part of our worship to God.

To reach such goals would be to have a vision and a foretaste of heaven itself. We would be gathered into the worship of heaven that the writer of the book of Revelation foresaw: "There was a great multitude that no one could count, from every nation, from all tribes and peoples and languages" (Rev 7:9). What doctrine of the Church would allow us to be so universal in our worship of the one God? What event could give rise to such inclusive worship when strong pressure would have been placed on the first disciples to keep to the strict pattern of worship with which they were familiar—Hebrew in language, culture, and form?

My study of the doctrine of the Ascension threw new light on such questions. Through it I realized that it was the Ascension of Christ that freed him from the limitations of particularity—being a human person in a particular place, time, race, gender, and age group. At the same time the Ascension connected Christ to the reality of being human. The ascended Christ was the same person who had died and risen again. The Ascension event declared to the disciples that the Resurrection appearances were over and that they could now have a new relationship with the Spirit of Christ. This would be God's gift to them. With the blessing and command of Christ, and in the power of the Holy Spirit, they were free to travel far and wide to root the gospel in each new generation, place, and culture. The ascended Christ, free from the limitations of being in a particular time and place, would be present with the disciples wherever they worshiped him and whenever they called upon his name.

In recent years most theologians have concentrated their studies on the doctrines of Incarnation and the Resurrection. The cause for this may well be the secular agenda which for many years grew out of a scientific dogma that reduced all reality and existence to what could be seen, touched, examined, and established by means of the microscope or the telescope. Such dogmatism has long disappeared among the true scientists, but it still lingers on in the popular mind.

Some theologians have attempted to restate the doctrine of Incarnation using the new understandings of physics. They have emphasized the little we really know of the mystery of the created order. Like many scientists, they call for a new humility about the human knowledge of the universe. Such writings have made clear again the good news that this Jesus can be regarded as both fully human and fully divine, "one person in two natures," to use the language of the members of the Council of Chalcedon.[1]

This restatement of the doctrine of the Christian Church has been necessary to combat the constant temptation toward heresy in the common mind. Too often people think of Jesus as God in human clothing—God one minute and human the next, but never completely one or the other. Often people think of Jesus as a sort of superman. For them he is so much better than any other human being, but yet he is not really God. This is because in their minds God is too remote, powerful, and distant to ever be fully part of this world and human existence.

John Wren-Lewis summed up this view in a sentence quoted in Bishop Robinson's book *Honest to God:* "The commonest vision of Jesus was not as a human being at all. He was God in human form, full of supernatural knowledge and miraculous power, very much like the Olympian gods were supposed to be when they visited the earth in disguise."[2]

The Incarnation doctrine is vital for the worshiper in today's Church. He or she needs to know that the Jesus whom we worship does understand our human condition because Jesus Christ was born of Mary and in this fashion has fully shared the experiences of being human.

Other theologians have concentrated their study and debate on the Resurrection. They have asked questions about its historicity and its meaning. The debate has been full of passion, for there is no doubt that the Resurrection has been a key element in our Christian faith from the very beginning.

In one understanding of the biblical evidence, the Resurrection confirms that the divine nature was dominant in Christ. In these readings the miraculous takes over, bodies disappear, and strange apparitions do appear. In the light of this, some Christians see the Resurrection as the "ultimate" miracle, where the supernatural

---

1. This was the Fourth Ecumenical Council of Bishops, held in 451 C.E., whose findings about the nature of Christ were eventually accepted by most Christians in both the Eastern and the Western parts of the Church. It remains the basis of the Creeds and Christian thought today.

2. John Robinson, *Honest to God* (London: SCM Press, 1962) 66.

supersedes the natural. Other Christian theologians have dismissed the stories of the Resurrection and see it as the attempt of the first disciples to overcome their devastating grief at the loss of their friend and Master. The Resurrection for these theologians becomes simply a faith-event. It counters the profound disappointment the disciples felt as their hopes to see God's reign of peace and justice come to fulfillment through this Messiah were crushed by his death on a cross.

In this debate about the nature of Jesus, some contemporary theologians want to concentrate on the Cross, certain that it is able to be proved historically. In the Cross they find comfort for the agonies and tragedies of life. In such situations they would rather have a historical Christ, who had suffered and died, than one who had escaped suffering and, through a possible resurrection, lived happily ever afterwards with God in heaven.

(Attempts to explain the Resurrection have emphasized the "spiritual" nature of the risen Christ and have virtually dismissed any debate on the empty tomb or the nature of the Resurrection appearances in any bodily form) The risen Christ becomes the Christ of faith, and awkward questions are avoided. In such a schema the Ascension is both unnecessary and a nuisance. It is unnecessary because the risen Christ has already been freed from the limitations of earth. It is a nuisance because the imagery used in the Ascension events is seen as laughable. A Christ who takes off in the clouds like a space rocket, leaving a slim trail behind him and a bewildered group of disciples gazing upward, is not seen as helpful in the age of evangelism. In today's Church it is very hard for Christians to win credibility among a skeptical audience that has no real affinity with religious symbolism. So such thinkers want to dismiss the Ascension as an invention of Luke in his Gospel and in the Acts of the Apostles. Instead they want to follow the apparent position of John's Gospel, where the Resurrection and "Ascension" take place in an immediate sequence. In that way they avoid the difficulties of any bodily resurrection appearances and concentrate on the "spiritual" experiences of the risen Lord.

Why, then, do I risk the dismissal of my conviction about the Ascension by both groups of theologians and raise again the issues of the event and the doctrine? Why do I go against the grain and tackle such a difficult subject in this short book? The answer is that unless we connect the Christ of history with the Christ of worship, we shall fail to hold together the two essential poles of the Christian faith. (Christ must be both in time and beyond time.) He must have been in history and been more than just a historical figure. He must be both fully human and fully God. Only then can Christ be the object of our faith and our worship.

To achieve this objective, I have undertaken in this book a full review of the biblical material associated with the doctrine of the Ascension. This includes not only the description of the "event" in the Gospel of Luke and the opening chapters of the Acts of the Apostles but also the departure scene that concludes the Gospel of Matthew and the references to Christ as King, as Intercessor, and as "exalted in glory" in other parts of the New Testament.

From this review of Scripture comes a theological reflection on the meaning and the significance of the doctrine of the Ascension for today's Church. I felt that it was important to reexamine the statements about the ascended Christ in the Creeds and, in the light of my comments above on the absorption of some aspects of the Ascension into the Resurrection, to look at the relation between those two key doctrines. Any concept of Christ's current state of existence will incorporate new thinking about "heaven" and "humanity." These are examined in Chapter 4, which then goes on to draw out the relationship between the Ascension and the Parousia.[3] We can then face the question: ("Was the Ascension the end of the beginning or the beginning of the end?")

The Ascension of Jesus can be seen as the journey of the humanity of Christ into the heart of the divine God and of our journey in worship into the divine dimension of heaven. For in our worship we are never earthbound; we lift our hearts and minds up to where Christ is seated, symbolically reigning over the world. There he holds it tenderly in love as, through his redemptive power, it is transformed and renewed to fulfill the purposes of its Creator God.

---

3. The Parousia is the completion of all things through the final revelation of Christ. See Chapter 4, p. 81.

It is important, therefore, to consider the implications of the Ascension for the worship of God that we offer in today's Church. I share my findings in Chapter 5 under the heading "The Liturgical Implications of the Doctrine of the Ascension." I was greatly helped in forming these conclusions during my sabbatical leave in 1996. This allowed me to participate in worship in many places around the world, where it is offered with faith, skill, and excellence by those of many languages and cultures. I spent Good Friday and Easter at Soweto, the African townships on the edge of Johannesburg; part of the summer term at Christ Church, Oxford; the feast of the Ascension itself with the Taizé community in France; Pentecost at Assisi; a week in the autumn in various centers in Israel; and a short time in Toronto, Washington, and Los Angeles. This gave me many insights into the helpful trends in liturgy today and the importance of the doctrine of the Ascension in giving us principles on which such trends can be developed.

There are also vital implications of the doctrine for our personal prayers as well as the prayers of the corporate Church. In particular, in the work of intercession we must learn to pray "with the ascended Christ" rather than as sole pleaders to a seemingly reluctant God. Chapter 6, "The Implications of the Ascension for Our Personal Prayers," first began as a memorial lecture given in Wellington, New Zealand, in May 1998, and later was published as an article in the November 1998 edition of the journal *Worship,* with the title "Praying with the Ascended Christ." I am glad to have the opportunity in this book to extend my thinking with the extra space available.

Ever since my first interest in the Ascension during the preparation for a lecture tour of Canada and England in 1990 on inclusive worship, ministry, and baptism, I have been invited to give the sermon in various locations on Ascension Day. I have included my understanding of the implications of the Ascension doctrine for preaching in Chapter 7. This attempts to help preachers disperse the wrong clouds associated with the Ascension and provides two examples of the type of sermon that shows the implications of the Ascension for today's Church.

In Chapter 8 I take a look at some practical implications for worship as we begin the new millennium, and from my experience draw out the "signs" of today for the development of our worship tomorrow.

In my Conclusion I have tried to summarize some practical implications of the Ascension for our personal relationships with God and with our brothers and sisters who share the name of human beings. Unless our theology influences our daily practice, it remains the subject only of remote thought. The Ascension has given me not only new insights into the doctrine of the Church but also new ways of living my life with Christ in community.

The Appendix contains an important examination of one of the problems I encountered while doing the biblical research into the texts of the Gospel of Luke when compared with those of the early chapters of the Acts of the Apostles. This is a short article first published in the *Expository Times* in April 1998. After the research my mind was satisfied that Luke is not describing two different events or versions of events, but one event by the use of two different sets of geographical signposts.

I am glad to set out all this material as a contribution to what I hope will be a new, widespread debate about the importance and meaning of the doctrine of the Ascension for today's Church.

Let me begin with some background information to clarify some of the terminology I use in this book and lay out at the very beginning the premises on which I write.

BACKGROUND INFORMATION

The theme of this book is based on the premise that the Ascension of Christ:

- marked the conclusion of that period of time and space in which God in Christ was voluntarily restricted to the here and now of earthly existence;
- marked the beginning of a new period of time and space by and in which God in Christ opened a relationship with a worshiper that was not restricted to earthly existence but transcended such boundaries, so that Christ became our contemporary and "one of us";
- marked the incorporation within the Godhead of those experiences that are common to all humanity, so that it was

possible to say that God understood our human condition with inside knowledge;

- marked the belief that the Christ of history henceforth had a continuing position of authority and responsibility within the Godhead as the Christ "seated at the right hand of the Father";
- marked the beginning of the responsibility of the disciples of Christ to carry the gospel to all corners of the earth, so that it took root in every culture on the basis of equality in terms of gender, age, and race;
- foreshadowed the final return of God in Christ at the Parousia, the summation of all the created order at the revelation in glory of God in Christ;
- released the Church to worship God in Christ in a way that was appropriate to that particular culture and generation.

In this book the Ascension of Christ is referred to both as an event and as a doctrine. To try to clarify the difference between the two, here are some notes on each.

The *event* represents the action by which Jesus is seen to depart from the bodily sight of the disciples and to resume fully the nature of the Godhead. The timing of this event is some period *after* the Resurrection. The Resurrection event is recorded in the Scriptures as taking place early on the first day of the week following the Sabbath Day of the Passover—in the Christian calendar, early on Easter morning.

In the conclusion of each particular Gospel none of the four authors gives any precise timing for the Ascension event. None of the authors seems to regard such detail as significant, and the timing is mostly indicated by the final appearance of the resurrected Christ in the verses before the concluding passage. However, all four Gospels have a "departure" scene or imply an Ascension event.

Similar variations are found in the *location* set for the Ascension event. Some of the Gospel writers give a particular location: Jerusalem in Luke, Galilee in Matthew's departure scene; or they leave it implied as the same place as the one in which the Resurrection appearance took place.

The event implies that Jesus was "taken up into heaven," leaving instructions about the relationship between himself and the disciples, and about the task that they are to carry out now that "he is gone." It points forward to the empowerment of the disciples through the gift of the Holy Spirit.

The Acts of the Apostles uses the Ascension event as the bridge between the life of the earthly Christ and the life of the Church as the visible presence of Christ in the world. It places the Ascension in *time* at a period of forty days after the Resurrection and ten days before the next festival, Pentecost (fifty days after Passover in the Jewish calendar).

The Acts of the Apostles also defines the *place* as outside Jerusalem on the road to Bethany on the Mount of Olives. The reasons for this timing and location I discuss more fully in Chapter 3.

The *doctrine* of the Ascension refers to that part of the statement in the Creeds of the universal Christian Church (Apostles' Creed and Nicene Creed) in which it is declared that Jesus "ascended into heaven" and "is seated at the right hand of God." The former statement affirms that Jesus is no longer to be found in bodily form on earth. The latter statement refers to Christ's position of authority over, and responsibility for, the world, and his glorification as God.

My hope is that you, the reader, will share with me a new sense of clarity about the Ascension from what I write in this book as a result of my research and the reaffirmation of the work of scholars to date, and then be able to apply that learning to the needs of the Church wherever you live. Out of biblical study comes theology, out of theological thinking comes practical implications for our life and witness as Christians and our worship of God, and out of our worship and witness comes our respect for others who share our humanity. The Ascension event and the doctrine that arises from it cannot be ignored or dismissed without serious loss to our theology, our corporate and private worship, and our ethical approach to others. That conviction is my spur to writing this book and to my own prayers with the ascended Christ on behalf of the world and today's Church.

CHAPTER 2

Prelude: New Ways of Seeing the Ascension

The reflections in this book arose during a period of sabbatical study based at the Universities of Oxford and Birmingham in England. At the University of Birmingham I had the honor of being appointed a senior research fellow in the Department of Theology, working alongside the Cadbury professor of theology, Frances Young, and the senior lecturer in theology, Gareth Jones. Their reputations as theologians and the association of the university with the late Professor J. G. Davies, who wrote with such passion about the Ascension, drew me to that seat of learning. A friendship with the Reverend Professor Keith Ward and his wife, Marion, enabled my wife and myself to enjoy their hospitality at Christ Church, Oxford, for the summer term. There the library, the meadows, the spires, and the worship of the cathedral added their inspiration.

I therefore had the best of two universities to support me, and I am deeply grateful to all concerned. They provided me with an opportunity for worship and study in tandem. It was while in residence in Oxford that I could share occasions of worship. It was while under the guidance of eminent scholars that I could carry out the study and research. I want to try to combine these two aspects in this book. To help my readers to come to see the truth of the research, I begin with pen pictures of three worship experiences. They will allow us to learn both from the pictures of worship experiences and from the insights of the mind. The first two examples arose from observing closely the art and architecture of two places of worship at Oxford, and the third from spending the feast of the Ascension with the ecumenical community at Taizé, which is a little village in the Cluny valley near the town of Mâcon in France.

Come with me and behold I will show you a vision.

Oxford is an ancient university of constituent independent colleges, founded in the fifteenth century and located in central England. It took up the responsibilities of higher education previously fulfilled by the monastic orders. The university is a society of scholars mutually supportive of one another, with the more experienced passing on their knowledge to the succeeding generation. Its colleges are founded as Christian communities that worship and eat together as the necessary fellowship for study, research, and knowledge. The library, the dining hall, and the chapel were designed as the three buildings to support these endeavors.

As some of the colleges expanded over the years, their chapels have been enlarged and rebuilt. In Queen's College, some of the stained glass from the earlier chapel was installed in the new chapel, which has now served the college for many years. One of the panels of this earlier glass shows an Ascension scene that is the subject of the first of the following reflections—Rising Above All That!

RISING ABOVE ALL THAT!

Gazing at the stained glass windows
in Queen's College Chapel, Oxford . . .

They had warned me about this window and its strange picture of the Ascension. Yet their warning only increased my desire to see it for myself. My reaction as a person of the twentieth century was one of shock and disdain. These windows with stained glass pictures had been made at the beginning of the sixteenth century for Queen's College. They were described to me as a series of graphically literal pictures of the events of the Incarnation,

Resurrection, and Ascension of Jesus Christ, and a final one showing the descent of the Holy Spirit at Pentecost. In the Ascension
window I was told that I would see the two feet of Jesus dangling
through the cloud as he was lifted up to heaven. In the Pentecost
window I would see little golden flames burning on the top of
balding heads of the disciples as the sign of the gift of the Spirit.

How could I ever find a sensible vision out of such nonsense?
Gazing at such windows week in and week out, I could not see
how any of the current generation of students could worship in
such a chapel. Everything else in the chapel was so beautiful, with
its eighteenth-century brass candelabra and lectern and colorful
Persian rugs on the marble tiled floor. Maybe one could learn to
shut out the unhelpful images as one shuts out the thumping
music that assaults our ears today.

Are we to react in the same way to the line in the Creed: "He
ascended into heaven"? Should we block it out, or start using the
Creeds less and less? With the picture from such a window in
mind, some declare that we should forget the Ascension as a doctrine, and more especially as an event. Then we would become
less embarrassed as Christians about these awkward doctrines.

But my gaze returned to the windows, and I let a smile calm
my intellectual anger. Like a good cartoon, the window has a lot
of truth to tell, as long as I was prepared to look for it—and smile!

If I believed in the Incarnation—that the Christ of eternity became earthed in the flesh of a particular time, being born of a Jewish maiden in the tiny country of Israel about two thousand years
ago—then I must complete that story with an ending true both to
history and to theology. If, in human parallels for divine events, I
have to speak of a journey to earth, then I must also speak of a
journey to heaven. Then this divine Incarnation would cease to be
bound to earth, dropping the limitations of our time and space,
and in the freedom of eternity and of heaven would take the
"proper" form of existence for God.

As we struggle for words to express the divine dimensions of
existence and think metaphysically (beyond the physical dimension), so the poet's mind will also give us a vision and produce
appropriate images: journeys, movements, clouds, earth, heaven,
departure, waiting, blessing, and hope. The truth can be told in

picture language just as effectively (and with equal difficulty) as the language that uses metaphysical words.

Gazing at these windows, I could see that in this study of the Ascension and its implications for today's Church, experiences, pictures, stained glass, and statues should be allowed to speak to us alongside the words of Scripture and theology. The students of liturgy give equal weight to both.

I looked again at this stained glass window of the Ascension in Queen's College and, with a smile, drew in its truth. The artist had drawn this picture with symbols in mind:

> *Clouds* were the way the First Testament often portrayed God's presence and activity. Clouds were said to be on Mount Sinai as Moses ascended and descended with the truth from God.
>
> *Mountaintops* were seen as the earth's attempts to pierce the heavenly spaces.
>
> *The upturned faces* were to show both the sadness of departure and the expectancy of blessing from the Divine.

Yet there was more truth to be revealed by this window. The mountains were not the small hills of Israel but the Alps of Europe. The men were not of the age or shape of the young adult friends of this Jewish Rabbi, but the faces and figures of the friends of the artist. They had bald heads and rotund figures and were very English! The city that was visible from this hill of Ascension was one that could be taken from a medieval painting of the buildings of Europe. The houses had many stories, and the towers were tall and slim. This picture, when you looked closely at it, combined the past with the present, the story of Jerusalem (or was it Galilee?) with the story of our civilization. The figure of Christ was hidden by the clouds, but if it had been visible, it would surely take the form of "one of us." What was true in portraying the friends of Jesus would in all probability be true for Jesus himself. They were modeled on the friends of the artist; so why not the face of Christ? Art had bridged the gaps of space and time, and the Ascension doctrine was already at work.

Once I could see through the clouds of confusion, here was a vision to behold with thoughtful care. The picture said it all, except that I still do not like the feet dangling from the cloud! That triggers my aversion to literalism, but I will not let that feeling divert me from its truth.

Let's leave the chapel and go out into the courtyard of the college. There in the sunshine is beauty and peace. The clouds race by in the sky and call on us to grasp the truth of the Ascension for us today.

* * *

Come walk with me now to another of the colleges, set among the spires and towers of Oxford.

Christ Church is the name of this college within the university, but its place of worship also serves as the cathedral for the diocese of Oxford. The origins of this church are earlier than the foundation of the college, and so it contains stained glass of different periods from the Middle Ages to earlier this century. These two periods of glass are represented in two prominent windows that portray the same picture of the seated Christ, but in a strikingly different way. They are the inspiration for this reflection: Christ Above the Heavens.

CHRIST ABOVE THE HEAVENS

The glass windows of the cathedral were radiant in the spring sunshine, their colors drawing the eye upward toward the vaulted ceiling, the stonemasons' parable of heaven.

The highest window over the main altar was built like a wheel in true rose-window form. In the center was the figure of the exalted Christ. Around him in a circle were the angels, all with their faces looking toward the Son of God in adoration and wonder.

Jim, the verger, being used to inquisitive visitors, recited for us the history of this window. It was a mid-nineteenth-century replacement for an earlier set of perpendicular east windows, which had occupied a larger space on the end wall. Dean Liddell (whose daughter was Alice, as in *Alice in Wonderland*) had spent much of his long rule as dean of the cathedral and dean of the college renovating the building which served them both as Christ's Church. This rose window certainly drew the eye, and hopefully the heart, upward to the heavens, there to find the ascended Christ, reigning as King.

Yet the face of this King was firm, even stern, as it stared straight ahead, looking into the heavens and over the earth. On his head was a crown. In his hands were the orb and the scepter. Here were the symbols of power over all the world. Here were the signs of authority. Every symbol seemed to mirror the power of the earthly sovereign of the time, Victoria, Queen of the Empire, transposed into the hands of the heavenly Christ.

Yes, Christ is King. Yes, Christ rules the world. But are these suitable symbols of his power?

This ascended Christ stared down at the world with a look of distance rather than love. In my humanity I felt fixed to the earth, not drawn to heaven. This Christ ruled over me with detachment, with little regard for my welfare. There was no look of compassion or even notice.

Above the altar was the Christ of the crucifixion. This cross told of the suffering of humanity. Here was defeat and the symbol of death. Around the Christ, hanging on his cross, stood his disciples, his mother, and his beloved friend in dignified support. There was no hint of power here. The head was not crowned even with thorns.

Yet the figure on the cross was still distant. This Christ did not look at me to draw me to himself in love and repentance. This Christ did not challenge my sinfulness and that of the whole human race. My vision did not come to life.

Wait! There were questions I must ask. Did the majestic Christ far above in the heavenly spaces tell me that the power of God had reversed this cross, so that the tree of shame ultimately shone out with glory and victory? No, I looked again but there seemed to be no connection between above and below. I was not drawn either to admire or adore, or to oblige or obey.

Was there nothing in such a great cathedral that might help me connect my Savior with my King?

We moved with the sun to another chapel whose altar was set to the east. "Come and see the medieval glass," was Jim's warm invitation to divert my obvious disappointment. And there it was, for those who had eyes to see. The tourist was attracted to this window because it contained a surviving picture of the murder of Thomas à Becket. In the sixteenth century it had been partly saved from the wrath of the king's soldiers, who had only been tall enough to smash the lower glass and to stretch up to poke out the face of the saint. The rest of the panel had been spared by its height, and the story was abundantly clear. I could see the king's men with their swords striking down at the figure kneeling at prayer. Here was another martyr killed for faith. Did Thomas à Becket, like Stephen before him, see the Lord in heaven as he died? The swords, the stones, the cross—none of these could stop the power of faith and love and forgiveness shining forth in Christ and in his martyrs.

The truth came together. There above the martyr's scene were the saints, then the angels, and then the ascended Christ in the very apex of the window, our glimpse of heaven itself. The angels looked down on us, calling to us in hope and encouragement, calling us to see the ascended Lord. There was no crown, for crowns belonged to kings who killed with the sword. No, this Christ had the face of a man with the kindness of God. His hands were raised in blessing and in prayer: the right hand stretched out the fingers in a sign of blessing, the left hand raised in prayer, open to show the mark of the nails. Here was my Lord, aware of pain, affirming that God's power of love shall reign. Here was my Lord affirming that despite the cruelty of humanity, God shall bless. This Christ is one with me in my weakness. In sympathetic unity he strengthens me in my struggles on my journey to heaven. The angels beckon me on. The saints and martyrs inspire me. I know that in the heart of God there is one who understands me and redeems.

Behold, here was a vision of unexpected truth. The angels sang, the sun shone, and we went on our way, rejoicing.

* * *

It is May. The sun is warmer and chases away the clouds from the mountaintops. The trees are putting on their summer green. The time is ripe for travel. It is Ascensiontide. We will cross the English channel and join the stream of pilgrims coming from the continents near and far to the tiny hamlet of Taizé.

Taizé is in southeastern France in the Saône Et Loire district of the Burgundy region. It takes about forty minutes by bus or car to reach the village from the nearest main center of Mâcon on the River Saône.

The village has become famous throughout the Christian world as the home of an ecumenical religious community renowned for the quality of its worship and its dedication to the goal of reconciliation and peace between individuals and nations. It aims to heal the new divisions of East and West, North and South. After the Second World War, as the community grew, there was much to do in Europe. Now the task is worldwide.

Under the guidance of its founder, Brother Roger, Taizé has developed as a religious community for men, so that there are now about one hundred Brothers from all the continents of the world. A separate Roman Catholic community of women religious, with its motherhouse in Belgium, has a center on the site and a community house in the next village on the same ridge. It provides care for women who may have a particular need and a house of hospitality for older folk and families.

The communities are dedicated to hospitality and provide a gathering place for pilgrims of all ages and races. One can stay for a weekend or a week in tents or dormitories, clustered around a large worship center and the places set for the fellowship meals. The worship of the Taizé community is especially well known for its musical chants and its profound silence. In the services the leaders use as many as possible of the languages spoken by those participating. Such worship is ecumenical in nature.

Continued on the next page

Although the worship center has been plainly built, in recent years it has been enriched by a series of small stained glass windows in modern style. These are set in one of the side walls. One of these windows depicts the ascended Christ in glory, in colors of blue, white, and gold, and reference is made to this window in the following reflection.

In the height of the summer holiday season some nine thousand people, mostly young, regularly gather at Taizé to join the community for their daily round of worship. They also participate in group Bible studies and in private meditation and prayer. There are opportunities for some visitors to spend a second week in silent retreat.

It is time to join the crowds and take in the sounds and insights of Taizé.

Ascension Day at Taizé

Raise your voices to the heavens,
for Christ has ascended on high!

The call of Taizé

High on the hilltop of the ridge above the ancient village, the bells began to call the Taizé community to worship. First there was a lone bell. Then the bells with deeper voices added their tones, another and another until the peal was complete. The notes of joy floated over the rolling hillsides, still shrouded with wisps of cloud.

On every pathway came the people to add their voices of praise to that of the bells. At first came the lines of pioneers, marking out the route to the large complex of a church that was really the size of a cathedral. The pathways soon became streams of living souls gathering with eagerness to add their voices of praise on this Ascension morning. This was a feast day in France and in most of Europe. The schools had closed, the holiday was kept, and the summer sun would chase the clouds and mists away. There was a note of expectation in the air.

As we entered the church there was already a carpet of people seated on the floor, showing every color of hair and garment. In the center of the building, edged by a low hedge of living green plants, was a long column of space that gradually filled with the white-robed Brothers of the Taizé community. They formed a visible pillar on the ground to hold the whole building of the congregation together.

The sounds of Taizé

As the bells continued their call, the Brothers and the congregation kept on taking their places. Any spaces in the carpet of people were spotted and filled. It seemed that the reality of the vision of the writer of the book of Revelation had come true: "And there was a great multitude that no one could count, from every nation, from all tribes and peoples and languages" (Rev 7:9).

The organ played a Bach fugue whose chords seemed to spiral, calming at one moment and stirring the next, anticipating the energy required for worship. The altar table was set before us, next to the Resurrection Candle. The shafts of light from the morning sun cast glowing colors through the slits of windows in the sanctuary and the roof above. Earth and heaven seemed to be meeting in this place of worship.

The organ music stopped and the bells finished their peal, and, as if reluctant to give way to the human voices of praise, each bell had a concluding ring or two from the energy of its final swing. Then all became silent—not the silence of a vacuum but the silence of anticipation.

Like the first piping song of a bird beginning the dawn chorus, a clear note from one of the Brothers started the service with the Alleluia for the Ascension introit. The vast congregation found its voice of adoration with the responsive "Alleluia, Alleluia," that word in praise of God that is the same in all the diverse tongues of Christendom. This word of the spirit was sung with joy. Firmer and firmer we affirmed the reality of our faith that Christ is the pioneer who leads us into heaven.

The people of Taizé

The carpet of people was a living demonstration of the truth of the Ascension. Every age, from the baby to the frail; every race, from the oceans to the center of the largest continent; both genders, well balanced in their numbers; and a multitude of languages, all used by people and leaders in this corporate act of worship, were gathered together in this church. Here the limits had been broken, and the circle of faith ever widened. All raised their voices together in harmony to praise God in Trinity.

This risen and ascended Lord was as close to us here as to those we had left behind in our local congregations spread across the globe. In this communion the obedience of Christ's sacrifice would transform our wills to be obedient to the will of God. We entered into heaven with joy, reconciled to God and to one another. We communicated in the language of love, which is the language of heaven. We were ready to give rather than to grasp. The one deep need we had was satisfied in meeting the ascended Christ.

The witness of Taizé

Since arriving at this worship our eyes had been focused on the icons and on the altar, with its burning candles and soft glowing light. As one of the Brothers rose and turned in the opposite direction, we too turned. With our eyes we followed him as he walked to a lectern to proclaim the gospel message out into the world. The ascended Christ had left his disciples with the responsibility of being witnesses to his words and to the truth. He commanded them to wait for the energy from on high that would empower them for this task. He promised them that God would give them such gifts. This promise was not only for the first generation of disciples; it was for every generation and every age until the Kingdom was complete. We, too, in our time and place, would be witnesses to God's power and transformation.

As the congregation turned, I had spotted a T-shirt on the back of a young man about twenty years old. It was glowing like a neon sign in the semi-darkness, proclaiming a statement so well known to modern travelers: "Nothing to Declare." Nothing to declare was the opposite of the gospel message that we had just heard: "You are witnesses of these things" (Luke 24:48).

As Christ's witnesses we had everything to declare. Christ had taken all our common experiences as humans into the heart of God and transformed the pain into hope, the struggles into confidence, the suffering into patience, and the hardness of heart into faith. How else could this microcosm of the world be gathered here at Taizé to share the feast of the Ascension? The prayers of the ascended Christ would gather up our prayers and knit them into a festal robe. We would be dressed for communion with Christ, for we were truly knit together as his Body.

The silence of Taizé

We professed our unity not only in the singing of the Creed and the peons of praise but in the profundity of silence. For two to three thousand people of all ages and conditions to enter into silence together for five to ten minutes was a miracle for modern society. "There was silence in heaven for about half an hour" (Rev 8:1).

Deep in meditation, active in prayer, relaxed in reflection—each used the silence as communion with God and a fellowship with one another without words of communication. There was a unity of purpose and a respect for one another about this silence. There was joy at this foretaste of heaven. In the silence we were aware of God, of our need for God and for others, and of the need of humanity for reconciliation and unity.

The peace of Taizé

After the silence the *Kyrie*'s voiced our longing for forgiveness. Then the words of absolution planted God's peace in our hearts again. We could make our plea and be confident of pardon, for the ascended Christ understood our frailty and struggle. Our High Priest, perfect in sacrifice, claimed our right to be renewed by God (see Heb 4:14-16).

The communion of Taizé

The tempo of the singing quickened as the cantor began "Laudate Dominum omnes gentes, alleluia" ("Praise the Lord, all you nations, alleluia"—Ps 117). As we joined in our praises for all God's mercies, a line of priests approached the altar. "The eyes of all wait upon you, O Lord." The eyes of this congregation focused on the table, then on the bread, and then on the cup. The language was French; the symbols were universal. Those who spoke in French spoke for us all, priest and people. We felt no distance, no withdrawal. Language was no barrier to participation in this setting of unity. Here, in this communion, time and space fell away and all was present. Earth and heaven were one. God and humanity were one. We were all brothers and sisters of Christ and of one another.

From the altar the Brothers scattered to feed the hungry for God. The Good Shepherd was our food and drink. Forward we came in streams that gathered to the wellspring of eternity and then turned again homeward with joy. Christ in us and we in Christ. Now we were to be Christ for others too. The Christ of worship called us to be witnesses for him in the world. We had "everything to declare": "The Lord is my light and my salvation— Ma lumière et mon salut, c'est le Seigneur, Alleluia" (Ps 27:1).[1]

The blessing of Taizé

The joy of our worship was almost tangible as the round "Jubilate Deo" pealed forth.[2] It matched the sound that the bells made at the beginning of the service. Brother Roger, the founder of this community, led his Brothers forth from worship to work for peace and reconciliation worldwide. From the base of the white-robed column of Brothers he came to the altar at the front, but he did not come alone. With him were a group of children whom he had gathered around him. As they reached the space before the altar, he blessed each one with care, and they skipped

---

1. Taizé Chant 64.
2. Taizé Chant 31.

away as if injected with life itself. In the worship on this Ascension Day the generations had met and become one. The aged man, with his white habit and white hair, with a skin almost opaque in saintliness, was young again in the children he blessed. His face had the smile of youthful trust and fervor for living. The simplicity of a child filled his trustful heart.

The children, too, had captured the maturity of age. They had learned the priceless value of silence in the presence of God. They had absorbed something of the singleness of purpose of those who had struggled through the multitude of worldly choices. They had imbibed respect and courtesy from the saint, who valued everyone as the child of Christ. They had learned that prayer was at the heart of being human, the prayer of purpose and the prayer of trust. Above all, they knew that there was a peace for them within God's creation and that they were beloved of God. They felt the blessing at the hand of the venerable saint, but it expressed the reality of the touch of Christ.

The light of Taizé

The congregation poured forth from the subdued lighting of the church into the bright sunshine, finding it hard at first to see on earth after being in heaven. But soon it was a single, new, two-dimensional world. We saw the earth with a new light. We had gained eyes to see heaven through the worship on this Ascension morning. Like a child we had been lifted high and carried on the shoulder of our Brother Christ to reach for heaven and to touch the Divine. Alleluia! Alleluia!

As one of the Brothers in the community has written: "The beauty of many voices singing together can become an entry point into what is beyond ordinary seeing and hearing, and provide a glimpse of what orthodox Christians like to call 'heaven's joy on earth.' An inner life awakens."[3]

---

3. Br. Jean Marie, "Prayer and Song in Taizé," *Ecumenism* (December 1996).

The prayer of Taizé

We were back for worship again in the late afternoon on this feast day, and for a third time after the evening meal. Worship was the reason why people had come to this place of pilgrimage. People came early to the services and stayed late, long after the multitude had gone on their way. Prayer and worship were at the heart of their new creation in Christ. The music, the songs, and the Scripture fed the souls of these pilgrims. They came back again and again, supported by the Brothers' pillar of prayer. Here was simplicity and also hospitality. It all looked so simple, but it was the summation of experience and struggle. A way had to be found for the generations to meet together in worship, for the divisions of tongues to be overcome, for people to be helped to stop the noise of the modern world long enough to leave room for silence and for God. And a way *was* found for youth to meet experience and maturity, for age to be invigorated by the enthusiasm of youth for worship and the gospel. Taizé goes on living Ascensiontide day by day.

The Ascension window at Taizé

In the Church of the Reconciliation an artist has created symbols in stained glass of the movement of God to earth and of humanity to heaven: Annunciation, Visitation, Incarnation, Journey to the Cross, Crucifixion, Resurrection, Ascension, Pentecost, and Transfiguration. The stained glass is built into the small and low windows that run along the aisle on the right hand side of the church. Most people would have to make a pilgrimage of intent to find these windows as they are not visible from the main part of the church.

The Ascension window is blue, white, and gold in color. The Christ is seated, clad in a blue robe that matches the sky and the stars that encircle him. The head of the Christ stands out clearly with a golden shape of the sun behind it. It fills the top of the window. The center of the window has a balancing orb of gold. At first it is not clear what this symbolizes. As you look again, the hands of the Christ can be seen holding it with care and carrying its burden. Just above it, on the blue robe at the place of the heart, is the outline of the Cross. Ah! Is not this the sphere of the world carried and transformed by Christ through the Cross? Here all the world's pain is turned to light through sacrifice. Here the world is carried with love into the heart of God, where it is part of the experience of the Divine. The stars in white seem to circle round as if the creation of God is always moving, radiating energy and purpose.

The vision at Taizé

I looked again and saw the face of Christ. It was a very human face, like the face of one of the saints of France. The eyes looked out clearly from the window. This Christ saw all that needed attention in God's world and should be brought into the Kingdom of God. Those eyes met mine and challenged me to be part of the healing of the world. I asked myself: "How will I take my part in carrying it, transforming it, loving it?"

Yet this challenge was not one of disdain or despair. This Christ was seated firmly in a position of authority and responsibility. He looked relaxed, holding the world securely, and the eyes were those of a person of depth who had seen within as well as beyond. This window called me to share Christ's trust in the purposes of God and in the fulfillment of heaven. My Brother understood me enough to be my Savior, and if mine, he was surely strong enough to save the whole world that he carried close to his heart. "Jesu Christe, O in te confido!" ("Jesus Christ, I trust in you!")[4]

With such experiences of a new vision of the Ascension through our worship, we can take hold of the Bible and through its pages see what insights it has for our understanding of the Ascension as an event and as a doctrine.

---

4. Taizé Chant 52.

CHAPTER 3

The Biblical Evidence for the Doctrine of the Ascension

I hope you gained many insights into the meaning of the Ascension in the Prelude. Now it is time to hold the Bible in one hand and some commentaries in the other. This should allow us to see how the various writers of the Scriptures portray their knowledge of the Ascension and the meaning that they derive from this awareness.

INTRODUCTION : A COMMON VIEW OF THE ASCENSION EVENT

Many people have assembled an impression of the story of the Ascension from various readings in the New Testament. The difficulty for us is that we associate one passage of the Scripture with another to build up a picture that is larger than that in any one biblical source. This is a reasonable approach if we can be sure that all the writers are referring to the same incident, but it may lead us to false conclusions where this is not the case. Here is an excellent example to illustrate this point in relation to the Ascension event.

Fay Sampson has included a chapter called "The Bible Story" in her small booklet for schools in the United Kingdom entitled *Ascensiontide and Pentecost*.[1] It gives an account of the Ascension from an amalgamation of references from various parts of the New Testament. Therefore it is a good example of the difficulty of assembling the record of the events from different parts of the

---

1. Exeter: Religious and Moral Education, 1986, 7–8.

Scriptures. The author has given her biblical sources as Matthew 28:16-20; Mark 16:19-20; Luke 24:44-52; Acts 1:6-11. Under the heading "The Ascension" she has written the following:

When Jesus was crucified the men and women who had followed him were plunged into grief and fear. For three years they had traveled the country with him as he taught about the Father and healed the sick. They thought that the Kingdom of God had come on earth. Now they had lost their Master. They could not understand what had gone wrong.

Then, two days later, Mary Magdalene came running to tell them that Jesus had risen from the dead and had appeared to her. At first they did not believe her. But Jesus showed himself to two others, and then to all of them. They knew joyfully that it was really true.

Jesus came to them many times. His Resurrection body was strange, but it was still the same Jesus they had known. Each time he appeared, he talked to them about what they must do next. But they expected they would always go on seeing him as before. They waited eagerly for the next time he could come to them.

Then one day Jesus led them to the top of a hill overlooking Jerusalem. He repeated a promise he had made to them before his crucifixion. He said that the Holy Spirit would come to them. He told them they must go out into the whole world and spread the good news about everything he had done.

When he had finished speaking, a cloud came down and settled over the hilltop where Jesus was standing. As it lifted into the sky, they saw he was no longer with them. As they stood openmouthed, gazing up after the cloud, they saw two men in white, who had not been there before, smiling at them.

"You people from Galilee, why are you standing looking up into heaven? This same Jesus that you have seen ascend into heaven shall come again in the same way that you have seen him go" (Acts 1:11).

Then they understood what Jesus had done. His work on earth was finished. He had handed over the task to them to carry on.

This summary is an interpretation of a number of the various texts that the author quotes.

THE NEW TESTAMENT RECORD

(For our purposes it is important to look closely at each biblical passage in its own right.) I have chosen to look at them in the following order:

- Luke-Acts, and the reasons for the different emphasis in the same writer;
- the Gospel of Matthew;
- the longer addition to the Gospel of Mark;
- the Gospel of John;
- the Pauline Epistles;
- the Epistle to the Hebrews;
- the faith statements in the first letter to Timothy and first letter of Peter;
- the book of Revelation.

Although the amount of biblical material referring to the Ascension is much less than that for the doctrines of Incarnation, salvation, and Resurrection, it is significant that the references for the Ascension are so widely spread among the various writings of the New Testament. The late Professor J. G. Davies of the University of Birmingham, in his detailed study of the Ascension, came to this conclusion:

(The witness of the New Testament writings to the Ascension of Christ is remarkable in its universality.) We have observed references to it in all four Gospels, in the Acts of the Apostles, in the Pauline Epistles, in the Epistles to the Ephesians and to the Hebrews, in the Pastorals,[2] in 1 Peter and in the Book of Revelation. We may confidently assert therefore that the inclusion of the words "he ascended into heaven" in the Apostles' Creed is amply justified by the evidence.[3]

2. By "Pastorals" he is referring to the letters dealing with pastoral matters in the early Church, which are contained in 1 and 2 Timothy, Titus, and Philemon.

3. *He Ascended into Heaven: A Study in the History of Doctrine* (London: Lutterworth Press, 1958) 45–46.

1. The Ascension in the writings of Luke

With this confidence in mind, I want to examine what for most people are the key passages in their understanding of the *event* of the Ascension of Jesus. They are contained in the Gospel of Luke and the Acts of the Apostles. The writer of both is commonly acknowledged to be the same. Whoever wrote the Gospel of St. Luke also went on to give a theological account of the spread of that Gospel through the power of the Holy Spirit in the first generation of Christians in the Acts of the Apostles.

The verses directly related to the Ascension event are these:

In the Gospel of Luke:

Then he led them out as far as Bethany, and, lifting up his hands, he blessed them. While he was blessing them, he withdrew from them and was carried up into heaven. And they worshiped him, and returned to Jerusalem with great joy; and they were continually in the temple blessing God (Luke 24:50-53).

In the Acts of the Apostles:

When he had said this, as they were watching, he was lifted up, and a cloud took him out of their sight. While he was going and they were gazing up toward heaven, suddenly two men in white robes stood by them. They said, "Men of Galilee, why do you stand looking up toward heaven? This Jesus, who has been taken up from you into heaven, will come in the same way as you saw him go into heaven" (Acts 1:9-11).

I have been greatly helped in the consideration of these two passages by the detailed study conducted by Mikeal C. Parsons.[4] He has looked at the reasons why the two passages are slightly but significantly different and has proposed a very sound reason why there should be the two approaches to the Ascension event by the same writer. In his comments on the two passages Parsons concludes that

Luke 24:50-53 while not an independent witness of an ascension tradition (on either text or source-critical grounds), may best be

---

4. *The Departure of Jesus in Luke-Acts,* Journal for the Study of the New Testament, Supplement Series 21 (Sheffield: JSOT Press, 1987).

explained as the result of an ascension scene which was transmitted through the tradition and compressed in the Gospel to construct a leave-taking scene along the lines of a biblical farewell account, and expanded in Acts by formal elements of heavenly assumption stories.[5]

The Gospel Passage

The emphasis as I perceive it in the Gospel passage is on the *blessing* by Jesus of the gathered disciples after he has given them final teaching and instructions. We can see the consequence of this assurance and teaching in Luke 24. In verse 39 of this chapter, Jesus assures his disciples that his resurrection body is indeed the true successor of the physical body that had suffered and died on the cross:

> Behold the hands that are mine and the feet that are mine (so that you will know) that it is me, yes my very self.[6]

His resurrection body is not a ghost but has flesh and bones and can speak and eat (24:40-43). His teaching takes the form of a short summary of the Creed of Christ:

> that Christ will suffer;
> and rise from the dead on the third day;
> and repentance and forgiveness is for people of all nations
> (24:46-48).

The disciples are to be the witnesses to such a faith and will receive the promised power from on high for this task if they wait for this in the city of Jerusalem (24:49).

All is ready, then, for the conclusion of the Gospel. What is needed is an ending that also points to a new beginning. As we read the passage we are asking, "What will Jesus do now, and will the disciples carry out the task they have been given?" Luke gives us the answer to both questions, but in a way appropriate to each portion of his total work.

In Luke's Gospel record there must be no delay in bringing the account to its conclusion. Jesus must depart decisively, and

5. Ibid., 62.
6. Author's translation from the Greek.

the disciples must depart obediently. Luke achieves this with an act of blessing and an act of praise. God blesses; humanity responds in praise.)The journey of Jesus, begun in the first chapters of the Gospel with the angels praising God at the birth of this child and continued in his tour of Galilee to teach, heal, and call a band of disciples, and seen as exodus in the entry into Jerusalem, there accepting the cross and grave, reaches its climax in the Resurrection appearances, of which this scene is the last in Luke's Gospel message. Here is conclusion and yet prelude to the new beginning. The bare facts are enough to fulfill this purpose. Jesus instructs his disciples and blesses them. The story comes round full circle, and the temple is full of the praises of God on the lips of faithful humanity, just as the skies were full of the praises of God on the lips of the angels at the beginning of the narrative.

As Parsons has so neatly summed it up: "The journey of Jesus is finally completed when he leads his followers out as far as Bethany and then departs from them. At that point, a new journey begins and is the subject of Luke's subsequent volume."[7]

The passages in the Acts of the Apostles

The Ascension passage also provides Luke with the necessary bridge between the two volumes. All the manuscript evidence points to the existence of two separate volumes, even though the story of the Christian faith runs on from the first to the second. The prologue to Acts refers to the first volume as containing the record of Jesus "until the day he was taken up to heaven" (Acts 1:2).(Acts then goes on to expand on both the teaching that Christ gave and the Ascension narrative, with new detail and new symbolism.)

Parsons continues with this comment: "Likewise in Acts, the ascension is recast as an invocation, providing the divine blessing on the Church as a pneumatic community, and on the outward expression of its mission to the world."[8]

---

7. *The Departure of Jesus*, 112.
8. Ibid., 150.

⸢The Ascension narrative in Acts 1:4-11 is therefore a dramatic opening scene by which Jesus commissions the disciples for their work and then leaves them decisively to get on with the responsibility that they have been given⸥ There must be no more returning to familiar places in the hope that Jesus might reappear with further and maybe different instructions. All that was required to complete the task had been given to them. They had been fully instructed. Now they could rest and wait for this divine enabling that had been promised to them and to all those who would come to believe in Jesus as Lord. As C. K. Barrett, the great commentator, has said: "⸢In Luke's thought, the end of the story of Jesus is the Church, and the story of Jesus is the beginning of the Church."[9]

In this passage from the Acts of the Apostles, Luke has expanded the symbolism of the Ascension event with two new features and two new theological points. The new features are the cloud and the two men in white robes. The theological points are contained in the passive verbs "he *was* lifted up" and "who *has been* taken up from you into heaven" and the reference to the return of Christ "in the same way as you saw him go into heaven."

The use of symbols

The use of the symbol of the cloud as signifying the presence of God is very common throughout Scripture. We find it in the Moses cycle in the book of Exodus (Exod 19:9). We find it in the Transfiguration story (Luke 9:34; Mark 9:7; Matt 17:5). We find it in the book of Revelation, where the seer says: "I looked, and there was a white cloud, and seated on the cloud was one like the Son of Man, with a golden crown on his head and a sharp sickle in his hand!" (Rev 14:14).

The cloud clearly symbolizes the presence of the divine, particularly when the writer wants to express the connection between "the heavens" and "the earth." This is an understanding of how clouds are placed between our space on the ground and the place beyond us in the far reaches of the sky, where in symbolic terms the transcendent God will exist. If we want to try to put words to

9. Quoted by Parsons, *The Departure of Jesus,* 193.

the symbol (which is not the most appropriate action for the scholar of liturgy!), we might say that Jesus leaves the space and time of earthly existence and assumes the space and time appropriate to the existence of God.

The second symbol is that of the two men dressed in white robes. Two men also appear in Luke's resurrection narrative and give an interpretation of the event that the women had observed (Luke 24:4). These two men are clearly the symbolic representatives of the divine message, and the fact that there are two of them simply affirms the truth of the message (compare "where two or three are gathered in my name"—Matt 18:20). The readers of Luke's account would have no problem in understanding the symbolism and neither should we. The explanation given by the two men answers our natural question as to what is the true meaning of what we have seen.

Lifted up

In our attempts to understand the writer's theology in this passage, it is vital to catch the importance of the passive verb. There is no sense in which Jesus zooms off into heaven on some spaceship. The action is the action of God. Jesus "lifted up" into the place of God. It is not within human power of Jesus to make such a move, nor is it the right even of the Son of Man to place himself in the position of power and authority. It is both the action of God and the gift of God. Professor Davies helps us to see this key point using references from Genesis 5:24 for the taking of Enoch into the presence of God; and from 2 Kings 2:1 and 3 for the assumption of Elijah; and, in the Psalms, the action of God:

> But God will ransom my soul from the power of Sheol,
>   for he will receive me (Ps 49:15).

And:

> You guide me with your counsel,
> and afterward you will receive me with honor [or to glory]
>   (Ps 73:24).

Coming again in glory

The other key theological point is contained in the reference in Acts 1:11 to the return of Christ in glory. We know from other New Testament writings that the Second Coming, better referred to as the "Parousia" (the revelation of Christ in glory), was an expectation in the early Church. This passage from the Acts of the Apostles would seem to record that such an expectation existed at the time of the departure of Christ. It was thought that if there had been an incarnation of God in Christ, then that must be an event in the new "times" that God had brought about in the world. Something new had happened. So the expectation was that the return of Christ must also happen within this current season of God's new time. Christ's departure at the Ascension balanced the Incarnation event, but the Ascension must also be followed by the return within this same season of new time.

The writings of Paul had already foreshadowed the connection between the symbol of the cloud and the return of Christ (1 Thess 4:17). The clouds are the symbol of the "go-between" God, and can be used both for the description of the departure and for the description of the return. As Professor Davies comments:

> [Consequently to St. Luke, although as we have seen this view was not shared by the other New Testament writers, the Ascension is a final parting which brings to an end the Resurrection appearances.] This fact makes it all the more appropriate as a revelation of the mode of the Parousia when Christ will come in His glory on a cloud.[10]

Brian Donne, in his study on the significance of the Ascension of Jesus Christ in the New Testament,[11] links the theological ideas of departure and return even more closely. He sees in this passage a clear message that the disciples will *not* have another appearance of the risen Lord until his return at the Parousia: "What is clear, however, is that the Ascension was necessary for the disciples to realize that this was the last occasion when he would manifest himself visibly until the Parousia."[12]

10. *He Ascended into Heaven*, 64.
11. *Christ Ascended* (Exeter: Paternoster Press, 1983).
12. Ibid., 8.

To the ends of the earth

The passage from the first chapter of Acts has set the scene for the record that follows in the rest of the book. It tells of the faithfulness of the apostles to the command of Christ to be witnesses to the ends of the earth. The Good News would be spread to the end of the earth and to the end of the age, not by the cleverness of humanity but by the power of the Spirit, which was given to the believers. In this record of the spread of the faith, a new figure who had not been foreshadowed by Luke in the first volume would have a dramatic impact: "Brother Saul, the Lord Jesus, who appeared to you on your way here, has sent me so that you may regain your sight and be filled with the Holy Spirit" (Acts 9:17). Did St. Paul receive a special revelation of the Christ in a post-Ascension form, or was it the risen Christ who appeared to this new apostle as one "untimely born"? Paul declares in his own writings, "Have I not seen Jesus our Lord?" (1 Cor 9:1) and, "Last of all, as to one untimely born, he appeared also to me" (1 Cor 15:8).

We will return to this difficulty when we consider the references in the writings of St. Paul, but there can be no doubt that however the appearance is to be judged, it was clearly recorded as quite exceptional, and thus may even reinforce the strength of the passage from Acts as pointing to a clear end until the Parousia of the expected appearances of the risen Christ.

Comparisons between the Gospel and Acts

Now we are ready to look at the Ascension passages in both Luke's Gospel and the Acts of the Apostles together to make the comparisons. In the comparisons between the two, Mikeal Parsons has highlighted the major variations. It is helpful to consider these carefully to suggest reasons for these differences. The main variations are in the timing, the site for the event, the activities of the disciples, and the absence in the Gospel record of the symbolism of the cloud and the two messengers.

Timing

As far as the timing is concerned, there is a major issue in the long separation between the Resurrection and the Ascension in the account in Acts. In the Gospel, Luke seems to imply that the events were distinct but that they happened on the same day; that was Easter Day itself. Chapter 24 of Luke's Gospel begins with the scene at the tomb, where the women approach with the spices to anoint the body, find the stone rolled away, and are informed by the two messengers that Jesus has risen from the dead. The women then inform the apostles of the message that they had received.

The scene changes at this point to the road to Emmaus (v. 13). This section also concludes with a report to the apostles, but this time the report is believed. It confirms their own experience of the risen Lord, who had appeared to them as well. The risen Christ then appears to them all, demonstrates his reality, and gives them full instruction and teaching. The timing of this, therefore, seems to be sometime late on Easter night. Jesus takes his leave and gives them the blessing.

The timing of the event is really governed by the reference in the Emmaus story in verse 29 to the evening and the meal together. (In the Gospel narrative Luke seems to want to bring the story to a decisive and speedy conclusion and does not make consecutive timing as much an issue as narrative timing) There is clearly a sequence: tomb, information, disbelief; new experience of the risen Lord, belief, confirmation of this on two further occasions; appearance to the group, teaching, commissioning, blessing, departing; return to the Temple in praise. The only time references are "at dawn" and "at dusk." The list of events, however, is much fuller, and it is not unreasonable to believe that the events occupied longer than a single day in actual time but not in narrative time.

On the other hand, the record in Acts gives the period between the Resurrection and the Ascension as forty days (Acts 1:3) and the period to the baptism with the Holy Spirit as "not many days" (Acts 1:5). This day becomes the day of Pentecost in the first verse of chapter 2. The explanation for this rather different timing in the second volume may well lie in the establishment, in the early Church, of Pentecost as the day when the gift of the empowering Spirit was bestowed on the restored group of twelve apostles (with the election of Matthias) and the community of the first believers. This left a forty-day period in which the many appearances of the risen Christ occurred and teaching was able to be given to prepare the disciples for the responsibility that they would be given to spread the gospel to the ends of the earth. Such a timing certainly makes good sense in the context of the fuller narrative that is set out in the second volume as compared with the first. As Mikeal Parsons comments about the opening scene in the Acts of the Apostles: "The disciples are presented in the opening scene as educationally, spiritually and organizationally prepared to undertake the task of worldwide missions to which they have been assigned."[13]

Site

The second variation between the two accounts is over the site. In the Gospel narrative the location is given as in the neighborhood of Bethany or toward Bethany (Luke 24:50). In the passage from Acts, the disciples "returned to Jerusalem from the mount called Olivet" after the Ascension scene (Acts 1:12). The authorities declare that geographically there is not much difference between the two locations, and it was good to establish this for myself as part of the pilgrimage to Jerusalem. Why, then, did Luke use a different name in the two volumes? Again, we must search for the clue in the narrative. The names will have different associations.

In the Gospel the association of the road to Bethany is with the entry into Jerusalem on Palm Sunday (Luke 19:29). By associating the event of the Ascension departure and blessing with the same place, Luke is able to indicate that the triumphal entry is matched by the triumphal exit. This time the Temple in Jerusalem will ring with the praises of the true followers, who have remained faithful in contrast to the rejection and opposition of the first entry into the Temple at the beginning of Holy Week. Again the narrative is brought to completion by the cycle of associations. The location of the Ascension event was clearly established in the tradition the author uses as being just outside Jerusalem on the route to the village

13. *The Departure of Jesus*, 195.

of Bethany. By associating it with that name, Luke is able to draw the readers of the Gospel into the resolution of the question, "Were the events of the story of the capture, death, and resurrection of Christ controlled by humans or by God?" The answer given by the Gospel is that all was in the purpose and plan of God. The purpose of the entry into Jerusalem by the Son of Man is to bring to birth the Kingdom of God. God's purpose is fulfilled because the disciples will take on the responsibility of being the messengers of the salvation wrought on the cross to people of both genders, of all ages, races, and cultures. The Gospel ends with this hope, and the record of Acts turns the hope into reality.

In the narrative of Acts, Luke associates the place of ascension with the name of the Mount of Olives. That is where Jesus turns prayer for God's will to be done into action. At the Mount of Olives the disciples' final memory of Jesus would be empowerment for service. This would replace the former memory of that garden where they had all deserted Jesus and fled. Like Jesus, the disciples would discover the power of prayer to fulfill the purposes of God. The record of Acts shows this to be true.

The activity of the apostles

The third major variation that can be noted between the two versions of the account is in the activity of the apostles after Jesus has left them. In the passage in Acts the apostles go to a "room upstairs" for the next scene (Acts 1:13). In the Gospel account the disciples go to the Temple to praise God (Luke 24:53). The Upper Room in the writing of Luke is the place where Jesus and his disciples, family, and close friends are most aware of the presence of one another (Luke 22:12). It is the place of the confirmation of the presence of Christ, and therefore the appropriate place to gather to reflect on his departure and promise. It is in this Upper Room that they are gathered to wait and to pray for the enabling power of the Holy Spirit. In contrast, in the Gospel passage the activity is one of praising God with great joy. As we have pointed out earlier, the note of praise and joy is found throughout Luke's Gospel as a major theme in his writing. Such words are therefore the most appropriate that Luke could have used to close the Gospel account.

Symbolism

There is also the variation in the use of symbolism. In the Gospel record there is no reference to the cloud or to the two men. The absence of reference to the cloud seems to be worthy of consideration. As I pointed out earlier, the Gospel narrative is highly condensed, and there is no need to introduce messengers to give an explanation for the event. However, in the whole of Acts the author uses a clear "dialogue" style, and the two men provide this in the Ascension passage.

Why does Luke use the symbol of cloud only in the account in Acts and not in the Gospel? The answer to this question may lie in the "view point" established in the two different accounts. In the Gospel narrative the focus is on the apostles. They are blessed and sent on their way. The third person plural "they" and "them" is repeated six times in the three verses (Luke 24:50-53). As the focus seems to be on the disciples, their blessing, and departure, there is no need for Luke here to go into the method of the departure of Jesus. Neither the cloud nor the explanation is required.

In Acts, however, the account is much fuller in style and elaborated for an effective opening to the whole book. Here the emphasis seems to be on Jesus and the method and meaning of his departure. In this passage we note the third person singular and the use of the personal name Jesus:

> When *he* had said this, as they were watching, *he* was lifted up, and a cloud took *him* out of their sight. While *he* was going and they were gazing up toward heaven, suddenly two men in white robes stood by them. They said, "Men of Galilee, why do you stand looking up toward heaven? This *Jesus,* who has been taken up from you into heaven, will come in the same way as you saw *him* go into heaven" (Acts 1:9-11).

With such emphasis on the actions of Jesus, it is right that the author should give space to answer the questions of method as well as meaning. As we have seen, the symbol of the cloud was well known as the bridge between earth and heaven, and the words of the messengers connect the departure with the expected return.

The tradition and its meaning

I find that such explanations for the variations indicate that the event of the Ascension was firmly rooted in the tradition that Luke followed. However, I suggest that he used the same event | *N B* for two different purposes in the two volumes of his work. In each he utilized the key ideas and language that would have been familiar to his readers and helped them to see the place and purpose of this event in the total record of Christ, as well as in the spread of his Church from Jerusalem to the far corners of the world. There some of the readers may well have been located. What they read may have answered for them the question, "What is the connection between Christ's departure from the earth and the arrival of the news about him in our town?" It also helped them to know that they did not need to try to go to Jerusalem to locate a new experience of the resurrected Christ. His presence was available to them in heaven, where they themselves could be through prayer and worship. They would know Christ in the breaking of the bread and the prayers rather than in the association of sites and places where he might have left a memory of his presence.

The narrative of Acts goes on to affirm the Ascension in two subsequent passages:

> This Jesus God raised up, and of that all of us are witnesses. Being therefore exalted at the right hand of God, and having received from the Father the promise of the Holy Spirit, he has poured out this that you both see and hear (Acts 2:32-33);

and:

> The God of our ancestors raised up Jesus, whom you had killed by hanging him on a tree. God exalted him at his right hand as Leader and Savior that he might give repentance to Israel and forgiveness of sins (Acts 5:30-31).

Therefore, it is the exalted Christ who pours the Spirit on the hearer of this Good News and brings to all the forgiveness of sins. In Luke's writings the Ascension is the necessary step to the delivery and reception of the gospel message throughout the world. In his two volumes he gives the various accounts of the Ascension with this truth in mind in a manner that suits the purpose of the two different works.

2. Matthew's Great Commission

Having considered the most detailed passages that refer to the Ascension, we now turn to consider the references in the other three Gospels before we consider the material in the Epistles.

For most people, the concluding verses of the Gospel of Matthew are known as "The Great Commission":

> Now the eleven disciples went to Galilee, to the mountain to which Jesus had directed them. When they saw him, they worshiped him; but some doubted. And Jesus came and said to them, "All authority in heaven and on earth has been given to me. Go therefore and make disciples of all nations, baptizing them in the name of the Father and of the Son and of the Holy Spirit, and teaching them to obey everything that I have commanded you. And remember, I am with you always, to the end of the age" (Matt 28:16-19).

This has been considered an Ascension passage, since the writer records it as the final departing words of Christ on "the mountain to which Jesus had directed them," and because the commission is parallel with that in Acts 1:8. There is also the claim by Jesus that "all authority in heaven and on earth has been given to me," and this is equal to the position of exalted power of the ascended Christ "exalted at the right hand of God" (Acts 2:32).

In the eyes of the purest biblical scholar, there is nothing in this passage that definitely connects it with an ascension, but only with a departure scene. It takes place in Galilee rather than in Jerusalem, in accordance with Matthew's preference for Galilee as the place where the disciples will see the risen Christ (Matt 28:7, 10). Although I admit that this is true, I do see strong connections which indicate that the writer of the Gospel may well have been aware of the Ascension tradition. The connections I see are these:

First of all, the scene is located "on the mountain to which Jesus had directed them." The symbol of the mountain is used in this Gospel in relation to the instructions to the disciples beginning at chapter 5, a passage commonly known among Christians as the Sermon on the Mount. The connection with Moses and the Ten Commandments is obvious, and in this final passage the author may intend the instructions of Moses to the Israelites before they enter the Promised Land to be in the mind of the reader (Deut 32:48–34:12). Yet there are other references to a mountain in Matthew's Gospel. One of these, I believe, is important for us to consider in relation to the Great Commission. This is the Transfiguration passage in 17:1-9. Here on the mountain, heaven and earth are joined as Elijah and Moses talk with Jesus (v. 3) and the voice of God comes out of the cloud, commanding the two disciples with Jesus to listen to his Son (v. 5). In this passage the "cloud" is a key symbol for Matthew, and if he intended the use of "the mountain" to refer back to the Transfiguration scene, then the symbol of the cloud may be inferred in the departure passage in Matthew 28.

An even stronger connection with the exaltation of Jesus must be seen in the claim that all authority is given to him. These are the words of the one who sits at the right hand of God and exercises divine authority. The event of the Ascension may not be included in the material in Matthew's Gospel, but the substance of the doctrine is certainly there. Jesus is exalted, given full authority, frees the disciples from the limitations of geography, and promises his presence wherever they will take the gospel until the Parousia.

3. The Ascension in the addition to Mark's Gospel

There is sufficient manuscript evidence to show that the original writing in the Gospel of St. Mark goes up to verse 8 of the sixteenth (and final) chapter. Verses 9 to 20 are known as the "longer ending." It is thought that these verses were added to the later manuscripts at an early date (first century) to complete what seemed to be a truncated Gospel record.

The earliest manuscripts show that by verse 8 of chapter 16 the original author of the Gospel of Mark had established that the Resurrection had taken place and that Jesus, through the medium of a young man dressed in white, had given instructions which were passed on by the women at the tomb that the disciples should go to Galilee to meet him there. The record, as the manuscripts show it, ends with the women fleeing from the tomb and saying nothing to anyone because "they were afraid" (16:8).

It would appear that when the four Gospels of Matthew, Mark, Luke, and John were being accepted by the Church to form part of authoritative Scripture, the lack of an ending in Mark's Gospel covering the period after the initial Resurrection event was seen as a deficiency. It seemed essential to make reference to the actual appearances of the risen Christ to the disciples; to show that Christ had given full instructions to the disciples to take the Good News to all and establish the Church in all places; and to conclude with the account of Christ's departure and a reference to the obedience of the disciples in carrying out the instruction they had received.

The longer ending of Mark's Gospel concludes with these verses:

> So then the Lord Jesus, after he had spoken to them, was taken up into heaven and sat down at the right hand of God. And they went out and proclaimed the good news everywhere, while the Lord worked with them and confirmed the message by the signs that accompanied it (Mark 16:19-20).

These verses mention both the action that Jesus was taken up into heaven and also the exaltation of Christ as seated at the right hand of God. Where did the writer find the material for such verses? We can certainly see a parallel in the Gospel of John in relation to the inclusion of Mary Magdalene as the first person to experience the Resurrection event.[14] This, I believe, is a superior parallel to that of the inclusion of Mary in the list in Luke 24:10. The writer could also have used the fuller accounts of the post-Resurrection and Ascension material we have looked at in Luke-Acts. Yet it may be too simple to see the passage as merely drawing on the material we have in the manuscripts behind the texts in our New Testament. We must not ignore the strong possibility that there was quite a lot of material in oral and written form circulating among the Christians of the first century that contained remem-

14. Comparing Mark 16:9 with John 20:1.

bered incidents about Jesus and the sayings of Jesus. These were probably "the traditions" on which Paul and the Gospel writers drew for the formation of their fuller and coherent written record of the gospel of Jesus Christ.

Whatever the way in which the author of the longer ending of Mark's Gospel drew on the work of others, he was certainly expressing the understanding among the first Christians that Jesus was taken up into heaven and was exalted at the right hand of God. His evidence is therefore seen as useful to those who have studied the Ascension. Professor T. F. Torrance has included it in his list of references to the Ascension.[15]

Brian Donne also comments: "Whatever the original conclusion of Mark may have been, we may confidently say that the Longer Ending does give evidence of a first-century belief in the Ascension as an event consequent upon the Resurrection."[16]

Although some dismiss this evidence for the Ascension because the verses do not form part of the original writing, I see them as affirmation that the early Church felt that the Ascension was among the essential elements among the post-Easter record of events. I therefore conclude that the Longer Ending of St. Mark's Gospel gives additional confirmation to the tradition that Jesus did appear to the disciples after the Resurrection and that he instructed them in their new responsibilities to "go into all the world and proclaim the good news to the whole creation," and that he was taken up into heaven and sat at the right hand of God. The latter seems a clear reference to the Ascension as both an event and as the basis of the doctrine held by the Church.

4. Three references to the Ascension in the Gospel of John

There are three references in the Fourth Gospel to the idea of ascension, although the Gospel does not describe the event at all.

---

15. Chapters 5–7 in *Space, Time and Resurrection* (Edinburgh: Handsel Press, 1976).
16. *Christ Ascended*, 13.

Instructions to Mary Magdalene

In his last two chapters the writer of the Gospel includes a number of post-Resurrection appearances of Jesus. The first of these is to Mary Magdalene and confirms for her what she had been told earlier, namely, that Jesus had risen from the dead. In the garden of the tomb she confuses Jesus with the gardener until he calls her by name and says: "Do not hold on to me, because I have not yet ascended to the Father. But go to my brothers and say to them, 'I am ascending to my Father and your Father, to my God and your God'" (John 20:17).

Some translations for the Greek verb *anabaino* give the English equivalent as "return" rather than "ascend." This seems far too weak to express the concept of "upward movement" always associated with the Greek adverb *ana,* used here as a prefix to the verb. There is, then, a strong case for seeing this reference as one which follows the tradition that Jesus ascended to the Father. Brian Donne has written: ("*anabaino* is always concerned with a rising upwards, and, as applied to our Lord's Ascension, means of necessity his rising upwards *from* the earth, as distinct from his being brought back to life *on* earth.")[7]

Given that this verse is in the context of a reference to the Ascension, it is good to reflect on why Jesus gave such a strong warning to Mary not to hold him or maybe touch him. There have been differences of opinion over the best way to translate the author's intention in using the Greek verb *hapto* in verse 17. The Vulgate translation had the Latin verb *tangere* ("to touch"). This is one possibility, and by using this word the Gospel author may have wanted to imply that it was not possible to touch the resurrected body of Jesus, at least not before the action of Christ's reunion with the Father was completed.

Jesus appears to his disciples in John 20 and 21. Although there is no record that anyone touched the resurrected body of Jesus the purpose of these passages is aimed at proving that the resurrected body of Jesus bears no resemblance to that of a ghostly body. In John 20:20 Jesus "showed them his hands and

17. Ibid., 9.

his side." Later there is the invitation to Thomas: "Put your finger here, and see my hands. Reach out your hand and put it into my side" (John 20:27). There is no record that Thomas took up the invitation. In fact, in verse 29 the words are: "Have you believed because you have *seen* me? Blessed are those who have not *seen* and yet have come to believe." This may imply that despite Jesus' invitation to Thomas, the resurrected body could not be touched. If so, it is possible to follow Jerome's translation. However, these verses could also imply that the body was touchable, and therefore "touch" is not a correct translation for the Greek. We must therefore examine the alternative.

Translators have also used the phrase "Do not hold on to me."[18] This would support the idea of not restraining the resurrected Christ from ascending to the Father. I myself give preference to this translation as the interpretation of the intention of the writer of the Gospel. It seems to me to be much more in tune with the reason given as to why Mary Magdalene was not to hold on to Jesus. It implies that Jesus was not yet freed from the restrictions of space by the journey of the Ascension. Therefore, Mary was not to cling to the earthly form of Christ. There at the tomb, the place where the memories of the dead were most alive, she must learn to free herself from attachment to Christ in that form and learn to find his living, spiritual presence in his ascended and exalted form in heaven.

In spirit and in flesh

I see parallels here with the dialogue between Jesus and the Samaritan woman over the proper form of worship in the new faith that Jesus is bringing to birth (see John 4:19-24). The earthly centers of worship from the past, whether they were at Samaria or at Jerusalem, must be superseded by the new dimension of worship "in spirit and in truth" (John 4:23-24). So the adoration and worship of Jesus as Rabboni (John 20:16) must be "in spirit" rather than "in flesh." John's Gospel implies that this is the only proper form of worship, and this must be offered to the ascended

18. For example, the Jerusalem version "cling to."

Christ. Mary Magdalene is not to cling to the old form but must wait for Christ to assume the new form "with the Father." Then and only then will such worship be in spirit and in reality.

This may also be the intention behind John's words in 16:16: "A little while, and you will no longer see me, and again a little while, and you will see me." Verse 10 has made it clear that the disciples will see Jesus no more because, as he tells them, "I am going to the Father." The new form of Christ will be the Spirit: "He will take what is mine and declare it to you" (16:14).

In John's Gospel, Christ has to go away for the Spirit to come (John 16:7). This Spirit is the Spirit of the ascended Christ which Jesus breathed upon his disciples during his second appearance after the Resurrection (John 20:22). John gives the time when this happened as the evening of the first day of the week (John 20:19), which parallels the opening phrase of the introduction to the Resurrection scene: "Early on the first day of the week" (John 20:1). John records a sequence for Easter day with the garden scene in the early morning and the appearance to the disciples assembled behind locked doors in the evening. In between, the impression with which we are left is that Jesus had ascended "to my Father and your Father, to my God and to your God" (John 20:17). Jesus, as portrayed in other Ascension passages in the Epistle to the Hebrews, is the representative of all humanity, to whom he is brother and fellow worshiper as well as truly divine.

John goes on to give examples of two further appearances of Jesus to the disciples. The first is to Thomas, one week later (John 21:26), and the final one is to all the disciples who have returned to the Lake of Galilee to go fishing (John 21:1-14).

In John's Gospel it is not clear whether these appearances to the disciples are intended to be seen as those of the ascended Christ or whether for his purposes the author does not see the need to draw that distinction. Certainly John does not include any record of an Ascension event, but he does seem to be very aware of the status of Christ as the one who has ascended to the Father. The Gospel regularly concentrates on examples of faith or disbelief in people rather than on a sequential record of events in the life of Christ. This is in accord with the purpose of the writing of the Gospel as stated in chapter 20: "These are written so that you may come to believe that Jesus is the Messiah, the Son of God, and that through believing you may have life in his name" (20:31).

Ascended into heaven

That John is aware of the Ascension tradition is confirmed by two other passages:

> No one has ascended into heaven except the one who descended from heaven, the Son of Man (John 3:13).

and:

> Then what if you were to see the Son of Man ascending to where he was before? It is the spirit that gives life; the flesh is useless (John 6:62-63a).

The first of these quotations is in the context of the dialogue with Nicodemus about eternal life. Nicodemus finds it hard to understand "heavenly things" (3:12). The dialogue calls for Nicodemus to understand the dimension of heaven. It is the Ascension, John implies, that enables us to picture Jesus as "in heaven" because he came from heaven. The Ascension is Christ's return to his former state, where the restrictions of earthly thinking no longer apply.

The exalted Christ

As I have examined carefully these references to the Ascension in the Gospel of John, I am convinced that John sees it as something that has taken place. Jesus is now the exalted Christ who is seated in heaven at the right hand of God. John points out that to come to know this truth, a person must have spiritual awareness, and only thus will he or she be able to continue as a disciple of Christ.

John's Gospel sees all truth from the dimension of heaven, to which the Son of Man has ascended to take the place where he was before (John 6:62), even though the author does not include any details of the Ascension as an event. This is in line with the tension in the Fourth Gospel between Christ as a heavenly figure and a strong emphasis on the humanity of Jesus. The Ascension falls within this tension, for it speaks both of Christ in heaven and the incorporation of the experiences of being human within the heavenly Christ.〔The Gospel therefore makes a rich contribution to our thinking about the Ascension.〕

5. References in the Pauline Epistles to the Ascension

It is not my intention in this book to enter into the complicated debate about the authorship of the various letters contained in the New Testament and referred to as "The Pauline Epistles." Suffice it to say that there is general agreement that Paul himself was the author of at least the Epistle to the Romans and the two Epistles to the Corinthians to which I refer. As for the other Epistles containing references to the ascended Christ, we can think of a possible joint authorship or even a collective school or group. Apostle and disciples were so close that the definition of the exact author is neither possible nor necessary for our purpose.

Some commentators refer to "secondary Pauline material" to make a distinction between the generations of the Christians to whom the letters were addressed, but I have included all references within the one section, for I simply want to examine what evidence there is for knowledge of the event and meaning of the Ascension among the writers of these epistles contained within the New Testament.

Resurrection and Ascension

In Paul's writings there is an understanding that the risen Christ is now at the right hand of God and there intercedes for us (see Rom 8:34). R. Bultmann argued from the evidence of 1 Corinthians 15:5-8 that "the resurrection of Jesus meant simultaneously his exaltation."[19] I agree that in the writings of Paul the two concepts are closely connected. However, I find that Paul does make some distinctions between the Resurrection as an

---

19. *Theology of the New Testament,* 2 vols. (London: SCM Press, 1965) 1:45.

event of the past and the current status of Christ as both resurrected and exalted at the right hand of God.

In examining 1 Corinthians 15, I note the differences in the tenses of the verbs. There Paul repeats the tradition that he had received (1 Cor 15:3) and uses the past aorist tenses in the verbs:

> He *was* buried;
> He *was* raised;
> He *did* appear to Peter . . . to the Twelve, to more than five hundred, to James, to all the apostles, and to me also (1 Cor 15:4-8).

But in verse 12 Paul uses the expression "Christ *has been* raised from the dead"; and in verse 20, "But in fact Christ *has been* raised from the dead"; and later in verse 44 Paul writes that this body "is raised a spiritual body." For me, Paul is distinguishing by the different tenses the completed act of resurrection and the ongoing current state of Christ as being raised to the right hand of God. This exaltation is part of what elsewhere has been seen as belonging to the Ascension doctrine rather than the doctrine of the Resurrection.

To my mind, Brian Donne argues convincingly that since Paul was a Pharisee, he would not expect the resurrection to be in any other form than "bodily." In all his references to crucifixion, resurrection, exaltation, glorification, Paul is setting out the full process of our salvation through the work of Christ, and therefore he does not rehearse the "prior historical steps" to his own experience of Christ. Yet he affirms that he had spent time with Peter (Gal 1:18) and was careful to preserve the tradition he had handed on to him (1 Cor 15:1ff.). As Donne says: "Paul's main contribution to our understanding of the Ascension lies rather in the *meaning* than the *mode*."[20]

Theology rather than history

I see it as quite understandable that Paul's chief interest should lie in the theological sphere rather than in the historical sphere. Paul's initial contact with Christ was his encounter on the

20. *Christ Ascended*, 17–20.

road to Damascus. The historical events prior to this were for Paul a matter of the witness of others. Paul would constantly refer to Jesus' death and resurrection as events of the past with meaning for the current believer, but he does not concern himself with the record of how these events happened. Such events would have been well known among the first Christians. What they needed was help to interpret what these events meant for their lives. Paul does this for them and us in fullest detail.

Paul tells us that because Christ's body has been "raised a spiritual body," we too will "bear the image of the man of heaven" (1 Cor 15:44). The Epistle to the Philippians contrasts the humility of Christ on earth, in his suffering and death, with the exalted status of Christ in heaven,

> who, though he was in the form of God,
>   did not regard equality with God
>   as something to be exploited,
> but emptied himself,
>   taking the form of a slave,
>   being born in human likeness.
> And being found in human form,
>   he humbled himself
>   and became obedient to the point of death—
>   even death on a cross.
> Therefore God also highly exalted him
>   and gave him the name
>   that is above every name (Phil 2:6-9).

Philippians 3:20 encourages the readers to believe that they too will share the citizenship of heaven and receive a glorious body like Christ's exalted body.

Seated at God's right hand

The Epistle to the Colossians confirms that Christ has been raised to the presence of God and is seated at the right hand of God:

> So if you have been raised with Christ, seek the things that are above, where Christ is, seated at the right hand of God. Set your minds on things that are above, not on things that are on earth, for you have died, and your life is hidden with Christ in God. When

> Christ who is your life is revealed, then you also will be revealed with him in glory (Col 3:1-4).

In these passages the author, in my interpretation, uses the verb "raised" to refer both to the event of the Resurrection (when the verb is in the past aorist tense) and the present state of Christ as being "raised" above (when the verb is used in the past perfect tense), where Christ is at the right hand of God. Other New Testament writers may well have used the word "ascended" or "exalted" for this latter meaning.

Contributions from the Pauline writings

With this link to the Ascension established, I see two very important contributions from the Pauline writings for this study of the implications of the Ascension for the conduct of worship.

1) *Intercession*

The first comes from the Epistle to the Romans:

> It is Christ Jesus, who died, yes, who was raised, who is at the right hand of God, who indeed intercedes for us (Rom 8:34).

This work of the ascended Christ in intercession is amplified in the Epistle to the Hebrews, which I will cover in detail later in this section. Suffice it to say here that the teaching on prayer in Romans 8 links the work of the Spirit in prayer with the work of Christ in intercession:

> Likewise the Spirit helps us in our weakness; for we do not know how to pray as we ought, but that very Spirit intercedes with sighs too deep for words (8:26);

and:

> . . . Christ Jesus, who died, yes, who was raised, who is at the right hand of God, who indeed intercedes for us (8:34).

For Paul there is a very strong link between the Spirit and Christ, so that the one becomes the equal of the other; note this example from the same epistle:

> I am speaking the truth in Christ—I am not lying; my conscience
> confirms it by the Holy Spirit (Rom 9:1).

It is the ascended Christ who intercedes and who pours out
the Spirit to intercede for us and in us. Through the Spirit's power
the prayers of intercession are indeed joined to the intercessions
of Christ in heaven. Christ prays in us and we pray in Christ. Our
intercessions form part of his desire that God's will be done on
earth as it is in heaven.

2)   *Unity*

The second important passage from the Pauline writings that
helps us to see the implications of the Ascension for worship
comes in this passage from the Epistle to the Colossians. After
stating that we have been raised with Christ, who is "seated at the
right hand of God" (Col 3:1), the author goes on to declare:

> There is no longer Greek and Jew, circumcised and uncircum-
> cised, barbarian, Scythian, slave and free; but Christ is all and in
> all (Col 3:11).

In this sentence we are told that the distinctions between race and
culture have been abolished in this new existence of heaven. From
the verses that follow, which deal with current ways that Christians must behave, it is obvious that the author is not speaking of
some future state for our worship but of the present reality. In
Christian worship culture does not divide us. It is not that culture
is unimportant, but that it does not cause any divisions and does
not exclude anyone. We are all equally included whatever the language or form of the liturgy.

These ideas are expanded in the Epistle to the Ephesians. The
period in which this epistle may have been written was probably a
little later than that for the Epistles to the Romans and the
Corinthians. The Epistle to the Ephesians in some of the extant
manuscripts does not have the location of "Ephesus" written in
verse 1. The letter may have been a more general one intended for
circulation among the churches founded by St. Paul's efforts.

God's gifts for maturity

It is helpful to look at how the Epistle to the Ephesians, which addresses the nature of the Church, views the Ascension and its implications for our worship. The key passage is:

> But each one of us was given grace according to the measure of Christ's gift. Therefore it is said:
>
> "When he ascended on high he made captivity itself a captive; he gave gifts to his people."
>
> (When it says, "He ascended," what does it mean but that he had also descended into the lower parts of the earth? He who descended is the same one who ascended far above all the heavens, so that he might fill all things.)—(Eph 4:7-10).

The connection in the author's mind is between the exalted, glorified Christ of the Ascension and the gifts of the Spirit, which enable the Church to function through these gifts, each appropriately given to different members. The aim of the gifts is that corporately we attain to the full stature of Christ (see Eph 4:13).

The Ascension is obviously taken by the writer of the epistle as a known fact in the Church, and the psalm that is quoted (Ps 68:18) can be applied to Christ. This Christ, God has seated at his right hand in the heavenly realms, far above all rule and authority, power and dominion, and every title that can be given (see Eph 1:21).

The implications for worship are that it is the ascended Christ whose Spirit enables the leadership of the worshiping community to function. This community is one body, in which all are fellow citizens with God's people and members of God's household (see Eph 2:19). It is such a united community that is encouraged to "be filled with the Spirit, as you sing psalms and hymns and spiritual songs among yourselves, singing and making melody to the Lord in your hearts, giving thanks to God the Father at all times and for everything, in the name of our Lord Jesus Christ" (Eph 5:19-20).

Summary

In the Pauline writings, then, we find clear evidence for the recognition of Christ as the exalted one, seated at the right hand of God, whose activity is to intercede for all people. This exalted

Christ bestows the spiritual gifts upon the members of the Church, enabling it to function so that all may attain to the measure of the fullness of Christ. Through his ascension he has gathered all people into unity, so that the distinctions of race or status are no longer relevant. All are reconciled as members of one body, the body of the exalted Christ.

6. The ascended Christ in the Epistle to the Hebrews

The references to the Ascension in the Epistle to the Hebrews are couched in terms of the exalted Christ, who is now seated at God's right hand. There is no mention of any kind of the Ascension event. However, the epistle is crucial in giving us insights into the nature of the one who is now our representative in God's presence.

The epistle portrays the exaltation of Christ as the lifting up to God of the true representative of the whole human race. Thus all the experience of being human is seen as being within the Godhead.

There are three key verses in this epistle that have shaped much of my thinking and enthusiasm for the writing of this book. There is also a longer passage which, once we have mastered its symbolism, will set out principles on which we can enter into Christian worship in our own time. The three passages, which are clearly identified as exaltation passages, are these:

> When he [the Son] had made purification for sins, he sat down at the right hand of the Majesty on high (Heb 1:3b).

> But we do see Jesus, who for a little while was made lower than the angels, now crowned with glory and honor because of the suffering of death, so that by the grace of God he might taste death for everyone (Heb 2:9).

> . . . looking to Jesus, the pioneer and perfecter of our faith, who for the sake of the joy that was set before him endured the cross, disregarding its shame, and has taken his seat at the right hand of the throne of God (Heb 12:2).

Humanity exalted

In these three passages the author of Hebrews establishes for us the view that Jesus is now seated at the right hand of God and has carried with him to this exalted position the whole experience of being human, especially that related to suffering and death. For the worshiper who has to cope with the inevitable sufferings of mortal life and face the prospect and reality of death, to have such a Christ at the center of the Godhead is an immense source of both comfort and strength. Our trials and sufferings are understood, not from an exterior point of view or through the reports of others, but from within the heart of God.

The author of the epistle is able to use a religious parallel that is obviously within the knowledge of his readers to reinforce this point. He refers to Jesus as "the great high priest" in chapter 4 and thereafter, and this passage is well worth careful study with the help of Paul Ellingworth's recent commentary from the Greek text.[21] I have also found George Buchanan's earlier work in the Anchor Bible series most helpful.[22] Here is the Anchor Bible translation for Hebrews 4:14-16:

> Since, then, we have a great high priest [who] has gone through the heavens, Jesus the Son of God, let us hold fast the confession. For we do not have a high priest [who is] unable to sympathize with our weakness, but one who has been tested in everything in ways similar [to ours, yet he is] without sin. Then let us approach the throne of grace with boldness, so that we might receive mercy and find grace for timely support.

The writer of the epistle, in this passage, brings together two of his key concepts: that of Jesus as the high priest and that of Jesus as the Son of God.

The great high priest

The high priest within the Jewish system of the Temple was the chosen representative of the people. It was his duty to offer

---

21. *The Epistle to the Hebrews: A Commentary on the Greek Text* (Grand Rapids: Wm. B. Eerdmans, 1993).

22. *To the Hebrews*, Anchor Bible 36 (New York: Doubleday, 1972).

the sacrifices in the Temple, particularly the atonement sacrifice that was offered once a year. He alone was able to enter the most holy space in the Temple, and all others had their own place for observing what was happening. Such a place was at a suitable distance, depending on one's station in life. Race, gender, and age were determining factors in according such rights to the different groups of people.

The word for high priest is one word in the original text and denotes an office, and in this office the concept of "high" is one of importance, not of space. Such an idea of importance is emphasized further by the use of "great." The writer of the epistle did not find this idea in the text of the psalms he was quoting. He introduced it here to highlight the superior status that he believes Jesus has, compared with even the most important human figure known to his readers in their experience of the relationship between humanity and God.

The writer declares that the great high priest is also the Son of God. By this he shows that the divine and the human are fully at one within the one man/God, who is Jesus. In this one person there is no inequality. The human and divine are in complete dialogue and harmony. Therefore in Christ humanity can approach God with full confidence. The sacrifice, already offered by Christ, will unite both in true fellowship, since the "will" of the one will be the "purpose" of the other. Each will give to the other what is right and proper. Humanity will give honor, praise, and adoration to God; God will give grace, mercy, and ongoing strength to humanity through Christ.

The phrase that most obviously refers to the Ascension of Christ occurs immediately after the mention of the high priest: "[who] has gone through the heavens." On this phrase George Buchanan has commented: "The affirmation that Jesus had 'gone through the heavens' expressed his (the writer of the Epistle's) belief in his ascension, but it was couched in terms of sacrifice in the temple."[23] In the Temple the sacrifice was burned at an altar, and the smoke from the fire and the offering passed up into the sky, and this was seen as "going up to God." Buchanan again comments:

23. Ibid., 80.

Smoke and clouds are very similar to the naked eye, so it seems that the smoke that went up from a bonfire formed a pillar which would let God come down to earth and let human beings send things, like incense and offerings, up to God. Since Jesus' crucifixion was interpreted by the author in terms of sacrifice on the altar, and since animal sacrifices were cooked or burned completely so that the odor could be sent through the column of smoke to God in the heavens, it seemed reasonable to conclude that Jesus too ascended into heaven, or through the various heavens, up to the throne of God.[24]

The writer of the epistle wants to establish that the sacrifice required under the Jewish law is no longer needed because it was fully fulfilled once for all by Jesus. The place of worship is now in heaven, where the high priest, Jesus, draws all people to himself, and in doing so we too are brought into the very presence of God. Heaven and earth are now at one in the space that belongs to God.

The Son of God

By calling Jesus the Son of God the writer points out the very close relationship that exists within the Godhead. The Son is the true and full image of the Father, just as the engraved seal will produce the real image of the original in wax. A son in this image has all the authority that a father possesses. The symbolism reveals for us what was the true position and nature of the man Jesus. He was not only our human brother; at the same time he was the Son of our heavenly Father.

That belief new Christians confessed at the time of their baptism. So the writer of the epistle is able to encourage his readers to "hold fast the confession." We might look for some amplification of this statement to clarify what confession is being referred to. However, the writer would not need to do this because his readers would be only too aware of the confession they had made at their baptism. Instead, the writer's objective at this point is to encourage his readers to maintain their confidence that they have made the right decision in following Jesus and being Christians.

24. Ibid., 25.

The writer knows the weaknesses that are always with believers—
the weaknesses of doubt, of the fear of being wrong, of the failure
to live up to the high ideals they had at the beginning of their faith
journey—in short, all the sorts of weaknesses with which human
beings are faced.

Can God understand such weaknesses, or is God so far re-
moved from the human condition that all such weaknesses cut us
off and distance us from God?

The writer of the Epistle to the Hebrews is able to give real
assurance to his readers and to us that we have Jesus Christ, who,
in the very presence of God, is able to *sympathize* with human
weakness. The word "sympathize" means not so much "to understand" as "to share the experience with" someone. Paul Ellingworth points out in his commentary that the word "sympathize"
has the stronger meaning of "suffering with" (as in the New Jerusalem Bible) or "feeling our weakness with us." He goes on to
quote Bishop Montefiore, in his commentary on Hebrews, where
he shows the importance of the Incarnation for this passage by
saying, "He sympathizes because he has, through common experience, a real kinship with those who suffer."[25]

No other religion makes such a claim for its God. Christians
at prayer have this unique confidence that within the heart of God
is an understanding, yes, a real experience, of the human condition. The writer of the epistle hammers this point home with the
use of the words "tested in everything." Such testing is in solidarity with the trials and tribulations of being human, and especially
with the trial of death. It is in our mortality above all else that
Jesus shares our human condition. Yet it is this mortality, this
death, which the writer regards as Christ's greatest offering and
which is a sacrifice that fulfills all future need for such a sacrifice.
It does not, therefore, need to be repeated.

The writer of the epistle draws a strong parallel between "like
his brothers and sisters [the Christian community] in every respect" in 2:17 and "tested in everything in ways similar [to ours]"
in 4:15. George Buchanan comments: "Just as Jesus had been

25. *The Epistle to the Hebrews*, 91.

made like the brothers in everything . . . so he was also tested in everything, in ways similar [to ours]."[26]

Humanity—Unique or common?

One of the questions that this study has raised for me is how far is it possible to say that Jesus shared in the whole of the human experience? He was fully human, but in that humanity he had to enter into the human condition in the particularity of one time, one gender, one race, one culture, and with a life limited to some thirty years. I want to take some time to explore this point, so I will simply raise the issue here, because it arises from this biblical quotation. I will explore some answers to the question in Chapter 4.

Our approach to God

The writer uses his argument up to this point in the passage to prepare for his key advice to his readers. Because of who Jesus is and because of what he has done, the disciple should approach the throne of grace with boldness. This is of tremendous importance for the attitude of the worshiper, now as well as then. First of all it is a *throne of grace*. God's rule is carried out with generosity and love. This passage rejects an image of God as the stern judge who rules with oppressive power. The graciousness of God is highlighted in the parables of Jesus and confirmed in this verse. And because this is the sort of God who "sits on the throne," the worshiper is able to approach with *boldness*. The word for "boldness" in Greek refers to the right to speak openly and without reserve. It was the attitude that a citizen could take when addressing the assembly of fellow citizens. The implication of the word is that in approaching God, Christians have the right to speak their mind and the right to expect to be fully heard, and still God gives the most generous of responses.

It is the ascended Christ who gives access to the heart of God and allows his disciples to have this boldness. As the true high priest, Christ stands in the very presence of God in order that the

26. *To the Hebrews*, 81.

faithful might stand there beside him. So they are able to approach God with confidence, knowing that they are not only heard but understood. The worshiper's respect for God and proper acknowledgment of God's supreme authority and power are shown by the position of standing, while God, the Ruler and Judge of all things, is rightly seated. All such statements use symbolic language to convey thoughts about a proper relationship between God and the worshiper.

Solidarity with Christ, whom we may call our human brother, allows his disciples to be one with him in knowing that God wants them to be in such a relationship; he wants to understand what they feel and have to contribute to the situation that is offered to God in prayer.

Such faith allows the disciples to have a very different attitude in times of prayer. They can move away from the feeling that they cannot possibly contribute anything to the outcome of the dialogue with God. If the picture of God is such that God is considered immovable and even impassive, then the only approach to God will be one of remoteness and even fear. It will be like being summoned into the presence of the authority figure in our lives, one before whom we feel powerless and intimidated. No one will want to enter into the presence of that sort of God or will only do so out of a greater fear that something worse will happen if he or she does not "face up to things." Such attitudes are childlike in the extreme and are certainly not informed by the biblical revelations of the true nature of God as found in Christ. There is no sense of delight or fulfillment in such an attitude to prayer.

This passage gives a very different picture of God and encourages an approach to God based on the images portrayed in these verses.

God's response

The writer finishes the passage by describing the response that can be expected from God. First, those at prayer can expect to receive *mercy*. Their weaknesses will not be held against them, and sins and failures will be forgiven. As the passage has made reference to the high priest, so the writer has raised the expectation in the mind of the reader that an understanding of atonement will be set forth. The writer must answer the question, "What happens if we sin?" He foreshadows fuller treatment of the topic later in the epistle by declaring here that we will receive mercy, and this clearly implies forgiveness.

The second response that the disciple can expect is *grace for timely support.* On the journey of faith each Christian looks not only for forgiveness of past failure but also for strength to carry on the journey. The need is for support and help in the appropriate form and at the appropriate time. Such support God is ready to give with a generous heart. As Paul Ellingworth states in commenting on this verse: "The throne of grace is where God sits (not where Jesus sits), and from his throne God dispenses to the penitent not justice, but free undeserved pardon . . . and the continuance of divine favor to assist him whenever need arises."[27]

Such is the work of Jesus as high priest that Christians are empowered for their journey to heaven by his prayers and his presence before God as their representative, understanding the human condition and assuring them that the generosity of God will be poured out for their assistance.

The writer of this epistle has added richly to our understanding of the implications of the Ascension of Christ for Christian worship and has raised some questions that I will address in Chapter 5.

7. The Ascension in the faith statements in 1 Timothy and 1 Peter

In the letters known as the Pastorals, the writer is obviously addressing the situation where the Church has reached a stage of substantial growth. It now needs advice about the best way for it to be organized and about the qualities needed in its leadership for such growth to be sustained. The writer of 1 Timothy advises on the qualities of life that should be found in a Christian leader and then adds a general statement about Christ, which could well be a short formula of faith.

27. *The Epistle to the Hebrews,* 92.

> Without any doubt, the mystery of our religion is great:
>> He was revealed in flesh,
>>> vindicated in spirit,
>>>> seen by angels,
>> proclaimed among Gentiles,
>>> believed in throughout the world,
>>>> taken up in glory (1 Tim 3:16).

1 Timothy: "Taken up in glory"

The inclusion of the phrase "taken up in glory" shows that in the early Church the doctrine of the ascended Christ was included among those that formed part of the expressions of faith as a member of the Church. Because of its poetic form, this passage is either a hymn or a confession of faith—something like an early creed. The Ascension of Christ is implied by the verb "was taken up." We have noted already the importance of the preposition *ana* in the composition of a Greek word, with its implication of movement upward. We also have in this verb the concept of being taken into the presence of God, which was part of the story of the "taking up" of Elijah in the First Testament. The phrase "taken up in glory" comes as the climax of this creedal hymn and states the belief that the current place where Christ is located is "in glory."

The phrase is one that is used also in the Epistle to the Hebrews (1:3) and is connected with the presence of God and with the image of light radiating from the presence of God. It is an image that has inspired numerous artists in the Church to picture Christ as seated in such glory and gazing out into the world he saved.

Used at the end of the creedal form, the Ascension brings the "movement" of God in full circle. The words "He was revealed in flesh" are balanced by the faith that Christ was "taken up in glory."

1 Peter: "Christ's entry into heaven"

A similar type of faith statement is contained in the First Epistle of Peter. This epistle is commonly regarded as addressed to those who were preparing for initiation into the Church. It contains teaching about Christ and would form part of the instruction before baptism. The epistle has a mixture of moral instruction as to how Christians should live as well as instruction about what Christians should believe. In chapter 3 the writer makes a number of statements about Christ as Lord:

> Sanctify Christ as Lord (v. 15).
> For Christ also suffered for sins . . . . He was put to death in the flesh, but made alive in the spirit . . . (v. 18).
> Baptism . . . now saves you . . .
> through the resurrection of Jesus Christ (v. 21).

and concludes with the verse:

> who has gone into heaven and is the right hand of God,
> with angels, authorities, and powers made subject to him (v. 22).

This indicates that such a belief was current in the teaching of the early Church and that Christ's entry into heaven was the climax of the work of Jesus as Lord. The concepts of Ascension, exaltation, and power to rule are all contained in this teaching and provide the Church with further material for the development of its doctrines.

8. The vision of heaven in the book of Revelation

Some brief references to the final book in the New Testament bring to a close this examination of the biblical references and help us to understand the place of the ascended Christ in the Scriptures. The book of Revelation does not refer to the Ascension itself, but in his visions the writer indicates that heaven is the place where Christ reigns in glory. There are three passages that illustrate the relationship between God and Christ in the writer's visions.

The throne

In the first passage the writer describes his vision of heaven and says that he sees "one seated on the throne," who is described as "the Lord God the Almighty" (Rev 4:2 and 8). The writer also sees a Lamb standing at the center of the throne (Rev 5:6).

We have seen the explanations of these symbolic positions in our survey of the material in the Epistle to the Hebrews. It is important to note again that the relationship between God on the throne and the Lamb recognizes that the Lamb is representative of humanity and therefore is standing. The fact that the Lamb is at the center of the throne implies that Christ is within the orbit of authority. At the least it implies a very close relationship between God and Christ.

This second passage is important for its implications for worship:

> Then I heard every creature in heaven and on earth . . . singing,
>   "To the one seated on the throne and to the Lamb
>   be blessing and honor and glory and might
>   forever and ever!" (Rev 5:13).

Here assurance is given that Christians can offer worship both to God and to Christ, for both are worthy of our praises. The exalted Christ is so closely intertwined with the God who sits on the throne that both can be praised equally.

The clouds

I have referred to the third passage previously in this section, as it includes the symbolic use of the cloud. This points to a strong connection in the mind of the writer with the Ascension. The particular verse reads like this:

> Then I looked, and there was a white cloud, and seated on the cloud was one like the Son of Man, with a golden crown on his head, and a sharp sickle in his hand! (Rev 14:14).

In this passage there are further similarities to the writings in the Epistle to the Hebrews. The one who is crowned is the one who has shared the life of humanity. The Son of Man from the writings of the Book of Daniel is identified with both a figure who represents humanity and a figure who is given full authority and power in the presence of God:

> As I watched in the night visions,
>   I saw one like a human being
>   coming with the clouds of heaven.
>   And he came to the Ancient One
>   and was presented before him.

> To him was given dominion and glory and kingship,
> that all peoples, nations and languages
>   should serve him (Dan 7:13-14).

Conclusion to the biblical evidence

This note of service that includes worship is an appropriate one on which to end this survey of the New Testament passages referring to the Ascension of Christ.

Brian Donne sums up my feelings as well as his own as he describes the Ascension in these words:

> Here we are at the very heart of our faith, in spite of all the mystery which surrounds it, for without the Ascension, a hiatus exists whereby the Jesus of history and the Christ of faith are virtually unrelated to each other. The Ascension is the essential link between the Jesus who walked this earth and the Lord of heaven; the Christ who entered our world of time and space and now reigns in glory in the eternal world; the Savior who died on Calvary's Cross and the High Priest who ever lives to make intercession in heaven for his people on earth.[28]

The doctrine of the Ascension and the event itself are variously described in the New Testament passages we have examined. At the conclusion of this survey I am left in no doubt that Scripture attests to its reality and the implications it has for the worship of the Church.

28. *Christ Ascended*, 25.

CHAPTER 4

The Theological Implications of the Doctrine of the Ascension

A number of theological issues underlie the doctrine of the Ascension when we see it as an integral part of the whole of Christian doctrine. In this chapter we will examine the relationship between the Incarnation and the Ascension, and set out some implications of speaking of Jesus as fully human and fully divine. We will then go on to look at the statements in the Creeds that Jesus "ascended into heaven" and that he "is seated at the right hand of the Father." The doctrines of the Resurrection and the Ascension are so closely related that some theologians make little distinction between them. We believe that we need to make greater differentiation between the two doctrines, and we set out the reasons for this at some length. This leads us into a discussion about the meaning of the word "heaven" and some new understandings of space and time in a theological sense. We believe that it is very important to highlight what is common to all humanity and not overemphasize the particularities of culture, gender, and age, and we give some reasons for this belief. Finally we examine the connection between the Ascension and the Parousia.

FULLY HUMAN, FULLY DIVINE

For there to be an Ascension there must first have been an Incarnation. So we need to ask ourselves, What was the nature of the person of Christ? Some people put the question as sharply as this: Was he God pretending to be human, or a human being pretending to be God? In answer to questions of this type, the Christian community by the date of 461 C.E. declared at the Council of Chalcedon that Jesus Christ was fully human and fully divine within the one united personhood of Jesus Christ, or to use the words of the council, *two distinct natures in one person.*)

This response to the question relies on the "both/and" principle rather than the "either/or" differentiation. When we set out to define something, we very often have to say what it is not as well as what it is. At times this leads us to think that something cannot be one thing at the same time that it is another thing. Within the Church we might say that one cannot be a minister *and* a lay person. However, there are certainly times when it is right to say that one can be part of the *laos*, the community of Christ, as well as being an ordained minister within that community. It is often appropriate to stress that a person can be *both* this *and* that rather than to declare that the person has to be *either* this *or* that.

Because there are occasions when we want to contrast humanity with divinity, it is sometimes difficult simply to affirm that the incarnate Christ was both fully human and fully divine. We say that human knowledge is limited and that God's knowledge is total. We affirm that God can be present everywhere, but that human beings are limited to a set time/space environment. We know that, on the one hand, human beings fail to achieve the highest goals they set for themselves and, on the other hand, that God does not fail to achieve the chosen purpose of the Godhead. We obviously have to take these differences into account when we say that Jesus was both fully human and fully divine.

However, Christian belief, based on the evidence of Scripture and the Church, is that Jesus was able to live fully as a human being and also be fully divine. By entering the human condition, Jesus willingly accepted the limitations of that existence but remained in his own personhood fully one with God.

To use an illustration that makes it possible to conceive of such reality, I draw on the experience of air travel. While I am at thirty thousand feet up in the atmosphere, I am limited in some things by that existence. I cannot walk far. I must be in a pressurized cabin of an aircraft. I need to take in a lot of water to prevent dehydration. Yet I am able to retain fully my own personality and all of my humanity.

In using this illustration I am not trying to draw parallels with the Incarnation of Christ. My intention is to show that even human beings can live fully in all the essentials of being human in such a limited environment. This encourages me to see the sense of the "both/and" statement in the paradox of the description about the nature of Christ. I can understand what Christian doctrine means when it says that Christ became one with us in our humanity at his Incarnation while still remaining true to his being as fully divine.

The Ascension, in a theological sense, is the other end of the Incarnation doctrine. Christ in his existence "in heaven" (that is, beyond the limitations we speak of as earthbound) is still fully human. Christ has retained the experiences of being human while still being fully divine. He did not drop his humanity in assuming the existence of divinity but retained his humanity *in a way appropriate* to the heavenly existence.

The Ascension doctrine cannot be discarded as unimportant if this truth is to be affirmed. That same "Word" that was expressed through the Incarnation of Jesus is now expressed in heaven through the ascended Christ. With this principle in mind, we can begin to see the consequences for us.

1. The first consequence is that as our pioneer, our forerunner, Jesus is able to point the way for us to follow so that we, too, may share in his exalted state in the very presence of God. Our future is bound up with his future. As Christ shed the limitations of earthly existence at the Ascension, so we will shed them and be able to enter into this new existence. Our destiny is not to be resurrected to this earthly existence—that would be to return backward, as if death had not brought to completion our mortality—but to move forward into exaltation and glory. There, to give substance to our personhood, we will have a body that will be appropriate to that state of being.

2. The second consequence is that we can trust that Christ retains the experience of being human to such an extent that he fully understands our trials and joys and can share them with us. In times of persecution this faith has been very important for the Christian Church. It is just as important in our times of happiness and joy as in our times of pain and testing. Our strength for living comes from the knowledge that Jesus retains the experience of living as a human being. Our dialogue in prayer with Christ is between two persons who fully understand the conditions under which humanity lives.

3   The third consequence is that we retain our hope that the end and summation of all things will also be "in glory"; that will be an existence where all find complete fulfillment of the purpose for which they were created. This is not to imply that all the created order will be at the same point at the conclusion, but that all will be perfect in the sense of having fulfilled the purpose for which they were created.

In our belief that Jesus was fully human and fully divine, we are affirming that the Incarnation of Christ was no accident but was in accordance with the will and purpose of God. Similarly, we affirm that the Ascension of Christ was a further step in this same purpose.

"He ascended into heaven"

This statement in the Creed makes it clear that the resurrection of Christ leads to his Ascension as the next step to his exaltation. The creedal statement attests what happened to the resurrected body of Christ and further affirms what the present location of Christ is. It acknowledges that the body of Jesus is not to be located within earthly existence. Whatever happened to it, it is not here (on earth), but there (in heaven). The action of the Ascension is seen as an action of God in restoring Jesus to the place where God dwells. This statement about the Ascension does not imply the method of this movement so much as the mode of Christ's existence. Jesus has ascended on high. We no longer look for him on earth as in the days of Incarnation or even as in the days of the Resurrection appearances. Instead, we lift our eyes to heaven, and in our imagination, inspired by such symbolism, we see there Jesus seated at the place of responsibility and authority.

The statements in the Creeds are supported by the writings of the early Fathers. Justin Martyr recites the teaching about Christ regularly in his works, of which this is an example:

> We say that the Word, who is the first offspring of God,
> was begotten without carnal intercourse—
> Jesus Christ our teacher,
> and that he was crucified,
> and died,
> and rose again,
> and ascended to heaven.[1]

Chrysostom, preaching about 400 C.E., points out an interesting distinction between the Resurrection and the Ascension and thus shows that he was well aware of both as part of the Christian teaching:

> In the resurrection they saw the end but not the beginning, and in the Ascension they saw the beginning but not the end. Because in the former it had been superfluous to have seen the beginning, the Lord Himself who spake these things being present and the Sepulchre showing clearly that He was not there; but in the latter they needed to be informed of the sequel by the words of others *[referring to the two men who spoke in the Acts of the Apostles passage to explain the Ascension to the bewildered disciples].*[2]

Clearly the Ascension was seen by the early Fathers as an important part of the theological statements about Christ, as it was an essential step in his journey to heaven. It was the prelude to the next statement in the teaching of the Church, as set out in the Creeds, which defined the activity of the ascended Christ.

"He is seated at the right hand of the Father"

The purpose of the Ascension is that Christ should take up the position of responsibility and authority that is the proper place for the Son to be. It is his by right because he is the Son of God. As Christians repeat the words of the Creed in the Liturgies, they are

---

1. *First Apology,* 1:21.
2. PG 60:28-30.

able both to acknowledge that Christ is in his proper place and also that it is the same Christ, who has shared our human condition and who has suffered with us and for us, that is now responsible for the governance of the created order and for our destiny. Jesus, who understands us and our human condition, holds responsibility for our welfare and has the authority to carry out the divine will and purpose. The power of the Son is complete and full, and there is no division of will or power between the Son and the Father.

The reflections I included in the Prelude on the stained glass windows depicting the ascended Christ seated on the throne, as seen in contrasting form in Christ Church and at Taizé, helped me to understand more fully this statement in the Creed. I began to see its deep significance when I reflected on the representation of the Christ, who governed the universe, and how the artist had portrayed the world in these windows.

In the window at Taizé, the Christ caresses the golden globe of the world. He carries it near to his heart. In contrast, so many other windows show the seated Christ as governing *over* the world, as if the world was to be pushed around. At Taizé, love and authority were linked together in a new way through this surprising symbolism.

To declare that Jesus is seated at the right hand of the Father is also to express the unity between the Father and the Son within the Godhead. There is no division of will or purpose. Worshipers cannot be misled into thinking that it would be better to call on the Son as their more compassionate Brother than to plead for mercy to a Father who is feared as a stern authority figure. Within the Godhead there is only one heart and one united purpose. There is no hierarchy within the Persons of the Godhead, but a shared responsibility and the exercise of authority by Christ on behalf of the whole Trinity.

The relationship between the doctrines of the Resurrection and the Ascension

There is a close relationship between the doctrines of the Resurrection and the Ascension, to such an extent that it is sometimes difficult to mark any differences, but there are distinctions between them, and these should be carefully defined.

The Resurrection doctrine states that though the boundaries of our mortal life are those of our conception in the womb and our death, yet there is life beyond that death. In such a life the uniqueness of the individual is preserved and a continuity with the earthly existence of the person is maintained, even though no mortal breath remains. To say that we are restored to life again is not to indicate that death is reversed as much as it is to declare that we pass through mortal death to a new existence, which is an even fuller measure of having life. This new existence can only be lived under the conditions of heaven. To speak in the language of doctrine, we too must ascend to the place where God exists. Our resurrection is a major step on our journey to heaven, but it is not the last step. Without resurrection there can be no ascension. Without the ascension we have not reached the goal for which we were made. Our future destiny is to be "in heaven," in the sense that there we will enjoy the presence of God and will be free from the limitations of mortality. There time and space do not bind us; death is past and cannot threaten us again.

As with the Ascension of Christ, the method of our ascension is not important, but the status of being with God certainly is. It is possible to conceive that we will have a body that is suitable to express our personality in this heavenly existence. The Pauline writings point us in this direction. However, we cannot penetrate that mystery beyond the point of seeing that it is conceivable, for we are still bound by the limitations of our human thinking.

The doctrine of the Resurrection concentrates on the victory over death and sin. It rightly affirms that our mortal death is not the completion of the purpose that God has for us. Christ's Resurrection assures us that we, too, will rise to a new existence, which is natural for those who respond in faith to Christ's offer of life. The victory over death had to be won for us and is presented to us as a gift out of the generosity of God. Easter celebrates this victory, and our baptism celebrates our acceptance of the gift and our commitment to live accordingly.

The Resurrection doctrine also affirms that the sins of humanity cannot overcome the power of the love of God. Easter,

therefore, offers us forgiveness, which opens up the reality of renewed relationship with God and ongoing life. The journey can
go on because the will of God is that we should not die in our sin
but find forgiveness and renewal. In this sense, Christ's Resurrection opened the way for us, and we can proceed toward the final
goal to reach the place where Christ is before us.

The next step on this journey both for Christ and for ourselves is the Ascension. By this, Christ and we leave behind the
limitations of our mortality and find our new life in *heaven*. Professor Davies summed up these ideas in these words:

> We must therefore go on to affirm that it was through the Ascension
> that this process reached its consummation, when the manhood, in
> indissoluble unity with the Godhead, entered upon a new mode of
> being and was liberated from its previous limitations.[3]

Professor Davies goes on to point out that it was not just the man-
hood of Christ that was taken up into the Godhead but in Christ
the whole of human nature:

> As applied to the Ascension this means that it was not the occasion
> of the exaltation of an individual man, but of human nature . . . .
> it was the taking up of human nature itself into the Godhead, being
> the completion of the redemptive act begun in the womb of the
> Virgin.[4]

The Resurrection marks the defeat of sin and death—that is,
the state of separation from God—while the Ascension marks the
beginning of life in the presence of God as an ongoing state both
for Christ and for all those who live in and through him. That state
we can define as being *in heaven*.

Heaven

For a generation or so the idea of heaven seems to have
lacked any attraction. Experts have been making attempts to push
back the boundaries of our knowledge of space within the uni-

3. *He Ascended into Heaven: A Study in the History of Doctrine* (London:
Lutterword Press, 1958) 179.
    4. Ibid., 180.

verse, and others have been hard at work trying to solve the problems of human existence between neighbors on the surface of the earth. To speak of heaven in metaphysical terms seemed to be irrelevant to either the realists or the visionaries of outer space, for heaven was a concept *beyond* space and time.

Iain Mackenzie, a canon of Worcester Cathedral, has recently returned to examine the concept of heaven in his book *The Dynamism of Space*.[5] In this book he stretches our thinking to conceive of two different types of existence, one proper to the being of humanity and the other to the being of divinity. To limit our thinking to that of our human state is to reduce ourselves below the level of that of which we are capable. We can and do conceive of more than the merely human. The philosopher throughout the generations has been as highly honored as the historian or the scientist, for thought is one of the highest achievements that can be attained by the human race.

If we understand the place to which we relate as human beings as our own universe, then it is possible for us to conceive of a place that is the sphere of God's existence. In marking the differences, we could speak of the first as *earth* and the second as *heaven*. Speaking in this way, we say that the earth is the mode of existence proper to humanity, and heaven is the mode of existence proper to God. We must be careful at this point not to go on to think that the two modes of existence are then so separate that God cannot penetrate earth and humanity can penetrate heaven. The implications for worship of that type of thinking are serious and have been the cause of much agony in previous times. Then people thought that the worshiper could not be in touch with God and God had no concern for mere humans. Our Christian faith refutes any such suggestion. The doctrine of the Ascension safeguards us from any thoughts in this direction. As Canon Mackenzie has written: "The ascension is the openness of creation's 'place' to have communion with the 'place' of God, the communion of creaturely existence with its Creator's."[6]

---

5. Norwich: Canterbury Press, 1995.
6. Ibid., 152.

The resurrection appearances of Jesus Christ are our glimpses of this new space/time reality. These appearances are both in our dimension of earth and in the dimension of eternity. We can imagine the first disciples saying: "We can see, but glory hides. We can touch, but only as a sign. We can apprehend, but not completely."

The Ascension is the sign that this new dimension, this new place of being permanently in heaven with Christ, is reachable by us even though we are human beings. Such a heaven is the light of a new dawn. It is beyond the veil. It is what will be when the mist rises and we behold the glory of the place that is not only God's place but ours.

Some might find this concept of heaven as a place proper to God rather difficult and would prefer to think in terms of activity rather than space. Canon Mackenzie has drawn our attention to the importance of the phrase in the Lord's Prayer in following this line of thought: "Your will be done in earth as it is in heaven." He writes: "Heaven is the doing of the will of God."[7]

The activity of those in the presence of God is to join God in willing and fulfilling the purpose and plan for the whole of creation. Using this language, to be *in heaven* is to participate in the divine purpose both for ourselves and for the whole created order. Such participation requires both prayer and active labor. Through the Spirit of God we can begin this activity in the dimension of earth and make it part of the dimension of heaven. Through the Spirit earth and heaven are bound in a single whole as we share in the fulfillment of the divine will and God's purpose for all creation.

Whether we speak of heaven as a place of God's existence or as the activity of God in bringing all things to their fulfillment, the essence of the concept is that beyond the limitations of earthly existence there is a heaven where God is and where God's will is carried out fully. The Ascension of Christ brings humanity into the sphere of heaven, and our destiny is to share the full presence of God and participate in the fulfillment of the purpose for which the universe was created. Once the worshipers understand this, there evolves a new approach to their own existence and a new responsibility for their actions. The Ascension doctrine opens up

7. Ibid., 159.

new vistas for them and brings about a deeper realization of the purpose of prayer and its consequential actions for responsible conduct in their daily lives.

The importance of being human

One of the key theological concepts that surfaces in accordance with this interpretation of the Ascension is the importance of stressing the common nature of being human. It is easy to stress the differences between human beings, whether on an individual or a corporate level. We have emphasized differences in culture, gender, and age so that these might be taken seriously. The move toward individualism arose when the biblical truth that each person is valuable in his or her own right needed to be highlighted so that the rights of the individual were protected. However, when it is overemphasized, a heresy occurs and the commonality of being human is overlooked. The individual then becomes God for that person, for there is nothing greater. The preferences of the individual become paramount over those of the community and are exercised as if there was no Creator to whom the person was accountable.

The doctrine of the Ascension is a helpful counterbalance to this distortion. It stresses that in the purpose of the Creator each person is joined "in Christ" to the community of all humanity, and "through Christ" to the whole created order. "In Christ" race, gender, and age are not the key factors behind our incorporation; the vital factor is our common humanity. This theological point underpinned the political position of Archbishop Desmond Tutu in all his activity in combating apartheid. He wrote in the darkest days of the struggle:

> If we could but recognize our common humanity, that we do belong together, that our destinies are bound up with one another's, that we can be free only together, that we can survive only together, that we can be human only together, then a glorious South Africa would come into being where all of us lived harmoniously together as members of one family, God's family. In truth a transfiguration would have taken place.[8]

8. Desmond Tutu and John Allen, eds., *The Rainbow People of God* (London: Doubleday, 1994) 117.

When the struggle was finally over, the Archbishop was able to offer this prayer of thanksgiving for the appointment of Nelson Mandela:

> Thank you, O God, that you have chosen this your servant to be the first President of a democratic South Africa where all of us, black and white together, will count, not because of irrelevancies such as race, gender, status, or skin color but because of our intrinsic worth as those created in your own image, as redeemed by the precious blood of Jesus, as being sanctified by the Holy Spirit.[9]

The importance of stressing the commonality of being human applies not only in the political sphere but also in the area of worship. Taken to its limits, the highlighting of the differences in the generation and the gender, the culture and the race, lead inevitably to a position where I can only worship fully on my own. My preferences are so unique that I can only worship alone and probably in silence, for no words are entirely satisfactory for my needs. However, the doctrine of the Ascension tells me that I always worship in and through Christ, forever in the presence of God. To worship "in Christ" is to be drawn automatically into the corporate body of Christ, where I can be uniquely myself, yet never detached from the other members of Christ living on earth and in heaven.

Christian worship always draws together people with differences—as Desmond Tutu would say, "irrelevant" differences—and helps them to see the glories of being fully human, bound in a common humanity. Worship helps us to see again the importance of being human. As Professor T. F. Torrance puts it:

> We worship the Father not in our own name, nor in the significance of our own prayer and worship, but solely in Christ's name who has so identified himself with us as to make his prayer and worship ours, so really ours that we appear before God with Christ himself as our one true prayer and our only worship.[10]

9. Ibid., 262.

10. T. F. Torrance, *Space Time and Resurrection* (Edinburgh: Handsel Press, 1976) 117.

The Ascension and the Parousia

The final consideration in this survey of some theological issues concerns the relationship between the Ascension and the Parousia, the final consummation of all things in God's created order. In one sense, it is right to see the Ascension as the end of the journey to heaven. There is a theme of completion of the work of Christ through Incarnation, redemption, Resurrection, and Ascension. The new humanity has come into being through perfect obedience and offering.

On the other hand, the purpose of God is not finally fulfilled until the whole created order has been brought to perfection. This will happen "at the last day," and in that sense there is a future yet to come and not simply an eternal present not yet revealed to us. There must be a future open for fulfillment to incorporate the element of choice and freedom so essential to the theological understanding of the relationship between God and the creation.

The Ascension can be seen as the foretaste and the assurance of the final summation of all things according to the purposes of God. Professor Torrance makes this point when he says:

> It is the ascension of representative Man in whom all humanity is gathered up and made participant in the self-offering, so that in his ascension Christ is installed as Head of the New Humanity, the Prince of the New Creation, the King of the Kingdom which he has won and established through his incarnate life and passion.[11]

This work has all been achieved by Christ, but it has yet to be accepted by all the created order. Until that time or within the bounds of the time that God has set for such acceptance, God exercises the same patience and restraint that Jesus showed during his incarnate life toward those who refused to accept him as Messiah. The fact that the Parousia is placed in the future does not slow down the urgency for the created order to respond to the will and purpose of God. To enter heaven is to enjoy the fruits of the Kingdom now, and no one would want to delay that joy of completion. In addition, once we have shared the vision of the purpose of God for the world, we have no desire to rest until we

11. Ibid., 112.

attain what we have seen as perfection for all. The vision of the ascended Christ draws us on to participate fully through prayer and action in the final redemption of all things from the corruption of self-decay. We long to see the whole creation share in the glory of the ascended Christ. That is our hope and that is our assurance.

Summary

In this consideration of the theological issues associated with the doctrine of the Ascension, we have highlighted how it helps us capture the key concepts of another dimension to our existence—that of heaven. This is the place proper to the being of God, and in it Christ exercises the authority and responsibility of fulfilling the divine will and purpose of the created order. We, too, have a place there in and through Christ, who is the fulfillment of God's design for all humanity. The Ascension doctrine points forward to the final summation of all things at the Parousia.

Such theological concepts have their practical outcome in the fields of worship and Christian activity in the social and political arenas.

CHAPTER 5

The Liturgical Implications of the Doctrine of the Ascension

In previous chapters we have referred from time to time to some liturgical implications that arise from the biblical passages connected with the Ascension and their theological implications. Now it is time to draw these together in a systematic way so that we can see the full importance for liturgy of the various aspects of the Ascension doctrine.

Heavenly worship

The doctrine of the Ascension reassures us that Christ is our access to the Godhead and that all our worship is "in" and "through" Christ. Because Christ has ascended into heaven, the locus of our worship is also "in heaven." The *Sursum corda* ("Lift your hearts to heaven") has been the classical call to worship from our earliest records. It sums up for us the call to raise our eyes to look on God with adoration and love and to lift up our hearts to offer our praise and thanksgiving to God as we seek to live in obedience to the divine will. These thoughts are the basis of all our worship.

One of the less helpful tendencies in the liturgical reforms of the last forty years has been to introduce symbol and language that appear to call God down from on high so that we can experience God "in our midst." As we shall see later in this chapter, the Ascension doctrine helps us to keep a balance between seeing God in Christ as "one of us" and Christ as "from the heart of God." Too great an emphasis on the Incarnation can distort this balance, so that worship is centered exclusively on the human aspects of worship—our concerns, our needs, our agenda, and our material world. Worship, unless corrected by the dimension of heaven, can become earthbound. The Ascension doctrine reminds us that there is another dimension to worship. We join Christ—rather than Christ coming down to join us—in the eternal nature of heaven, and there our worship is caught up with that of the angels and archangels and the apostles of every generation. As we explained in Chapter 4, heaven is not a matter of distance and place but of activity. Heaven is the sphere of God's loving power and will. In worship we can think of "heaven" as a dimension rather than a place far above us in the sky.

As St. Paul affirms, our citizenship is in heaven (Phil 3:20). In the same epistle Paul gives clear advice as to how individual disciples should live in their daily life on earth (Phil 4:2-3). This heavenly dimension of worship gives us a new perspective on our day-to-day living, and new hope and courage to live well in our material world.

Thus our liturgy needs to reflect this dual dimension to life and worship. The opening sequence to the liturgy should help us keep this balance. The gathering of the people has received full attention in the revisions of the liturgy in the period 1960 to 1990. This part was strengthened to acknowledge that worship is a communal activity, not simply an individual one. Within the Christendom of earlier generations, the worshiping community was firmly established through the social community. There was, therefore, little need to reestablish its reality when the community entered into worship. The deconstruction of the Christian community through individualism and the fragmentation of the unity of the community's faith make it necessary for the liturgy to provide an opportunity to establish a new worshiping community at the beginning of each service of worship. The worshipers have to meet their neighbors and retie the bonds of faith and love that they individually hold within an alien society.

In doing this new exercise, the other aspect of worship—the acknowledgment of the reality and priority of God—has often been overshadowed. The reexamination of the doctrine of the Ascension should help us return to a fuller balance between these two aspects of worship. We will make more obvious at the commencement of worship our acknowledgment of the presence, power, and reality of God alongside our affirmation of the community at worship. The people's response to the *Sursum corda* is an affirmation of their commitment to worship by entering into heaven with the ascended Christ and there acknowledging his lordship.

The word "Lord" has lost favor with some writers of liturgy because it was seen to stress a hierarchical view of the nature of God. Such thinking rebelled against dominance, authoritarianism, and any male imperial imagery. Yet the Greek word *Kurios* was used in the Septuagint as the spoken symbol for the unutterable name for God in the Hebrew Scriptures. The use of this word by the worshipers was a signal that they wanted to seize the opportunity to worship and adore the Creator God and to offer obedience to the will of God. In addressing God they proclaimed that they trusted God to strive for the best that they could possibly want for themselves. Such worship and discipleship are summed up in the human cry "Jesus is Lord." The doctrine of the Ascension summarizes the understanding of the early Church that it was "proper" and right to worship Jesus of Nazareth as being one within the Godhead. For a Jew to worship anyone or anything other than God was the greatest of blasphemies. The experience of the Ascension allowed the Church to feel at total ease with the worship of Jesus as God. Luke makes clear at the close of his Gospel that the worship of Jesus by the disciples allowed them at the same time to bless and worship God (Luke 24:52-53).

The doctrine of the Ascension will help the writers of liturgy in the new millennium to balance the recognition of the human community at worship with the acknowledgment of the worship of the Lord in heaven. They may wish to place the *Sursum corda* and the *Sanctus* at the opening sequence of worship and repeat these key responses at the beginning of the Great Thanksgiving Prayer for the Eucharist. If it is considered that there is need for a new set of words at the opening of worship, the Book of Revelation is an obvious place from which we can draw suitable phrases. It would be possible to combine words in verses 4 and 6 of chapter 1 to create a new opening versicle and response between priest and people:

> ℣. Grace to you, and peace from God,
>   who is and who was and who is to come.
> ℟. To God be glory and dominion
>   forever and ever. Amen.

If such a response were followed by a deep silence, and then a canticle or hymn of praise were sung, a strong opening would be formed that would balance the establishment of the liturgical community by mutual greetings and their praise and worship of God.

To locate our worship in heaven as modeled in the Book of Revelation encourages us to link our worship at this present point of time and our current location with the Church of all ages and all places. It will help our worship to be fully catholic in the true meaning of that word. Our concerns in prayer will be wider, and our faith will be supported by the faith of the universal Church. In many places Christians are now worshiping in isolated situations, even if they are not actually being persecuted, and need the aid of heavenly worship to strengthen their resolve to stay faithful to the Lord. Heavenly worship also assists us to see our current trials in the context of the wider perspectives of time. In the life of eternity such trials may be but for a moment. God, not our difficulties, will become the focus of our worship, and in God we will learn again to put our trust.

God understands our human situation

Alongside the knowledge that our worship lifts us to heaven is our understanding from the Ascension doctrine that God fully understands our human situation. This will save our worship from being otherworldly and a false route to escape facing our problems. Because of the Ascension we can be certain that God in Christ understands the human situation. Though this is always unique to the individual, it contains a commonality that makes it understandable across the barriers of time, age, gender, and culture. Human beings are made so as to be able to empathize with one another across such divides.

The life and teaching of Jesus stress the commonality of the human condition. Women and men approached him and were heartened by his response. The old and the young were attracted to him as one who understood their needs. The Jew and the Gentile sought his help and were not disappointed. The Spirit of Jesus, since the Ascension, has been equally accessible and responsive. There is no situation beyond the understanding of Christ. That is the witness of the Church of all generations and cultures.

This principle of the Ascension is at work in our worship. We bring our human situation to God and find a listening ear and a responsive heart. This encourages us to be real in our worship and to reveal ourselves as we are to God. Though our hearts are lifted up to heaven, our feet are firmly rooted to the earth. This sense of realism before God is essential for our relationship with God in worship and for the relevance of worship to our day-to-day life.

Our joys and triumphs, our sadness and failure, our sense of pain and cries of hope, our steadfastness in faith and our wavering in uncertainty—all form part of the agenda for our worship. One of the implications of the doctrine of the Ascension for the Church today should be an endeavor to find more appropriate ways within corporate worship for the expression of the actual human situations before God. The generality of corporate worship can work against the naming of the specific situation for the worshiper. When there is a major corporate situation, be it one of pain or pleasure, it is easier for the situation to be the proper focus of attention during worship. When the situations are hidden in the minds of the worshipers, it is more difficult to draw them forth and give them proper space before God. Looking back in history, we can see the way that individuals, carrying out their private devotions while the liturgy of the Church went on around them, were able to combine the focus on their own situation with the worship of the Church as a whole. It was not that the individuals were spectators and failed to participate, but rather that the individuals and corporate worship flourished in parallel.

The doctrine of the Ascension calls upon today's Church to make provision for ways in which worshipers can share with God the human situations that face them, and be reassured that God will respond appropriately. This is already done where there is an opportunity for the worshiper to share any special concerns with an intercessor in prayer. This may take place parallel with the distribution of communion or following the close of the service in a side chapel. However, it would have wider effect if there were some way of providing an opportunity within the service itself. The very nature of the psalms as expressions of the reality of the human situation makes some occasion in association with the saying of the psalm one such opportunity. Whatever practical solution proves best, the principle is clear: For worship to be relevant for the worshiper, there must be opportunity for the reality of the human situation to be revealed before God and for God's response to be affirmed.

The experience of blessing

The experience for the disciples at the departure of Jesus was one of blessing and empowerment, not one of desertion. This experience of blessing has formed a vital part of our liturgy. Our worship puts us in touch with the ascended Christ. Christ meets us within our human situation and empathizes with it. Having revealed the situation to God, we seek and receive the response of Christ's blessing of empowerment.

God's blessing brings the same joy, strength, and patience that the first disciples experienced at the Ascension. It is surprising to see that this was the evidence of the New Testament passages when we consider the reality of the situation for the first disciples. We would have expected the departure of Jesus to give rise to feelings of sadness, weakness, and impatience. The disciples were likely to be sad because the bonds of affection and relationship would seem to have been broken for the last time. We would have expected them to be weakened in spirit because they would no longer be able to rely on the presence of Jesus to boost their confidence and correct their mistakes. They were likely to be impatient because their hopes for a glorious victory would be dashed by the departure. Yet their faith in the final words of Jesus was such that they were empowered by his blessing to face the reality of the human situations in which they found themselves. Life was fragile and full of risks. Their conception of what was best would be subject to challenge and change. Many would listen with eagerness to the good news of what Christ had done, but others would declare that their claims that Jesus was the Messiah were blasphemy.

The disciples' experience of blessing was one of empowerment to face the situation as it was and transform it, but not try to escape it. Too often we look for God's blessing in worship to help us avoid the situations we face. Luke makes it clear that the disciples returned to Jerusalem, the place of the Cross as well as the Resurrection. In our worship the blessing of God equips us for mission and service in our daily living, with all the cost and rewards that are involved.

In worship the action of blessing in response to the revelation of our situation comes in a variety of ways. In Eucharistic worship it comes in the act of communion, in the words of absolution, and in the blessing of the faithful prior to the dismissal. In a healing service it will come in response to the prayer of intercession for healing and peace. In a confirmation service the blessing will form part of the bestowal of the gifts of the Spirit through the laying on of hands. In a marriage service the blessing will represent the action of the God of love in strengthening the pledged love of the couple that unites them in heart, body, and mind.

In a service of the Word it is important that the action of blessing be given due prominence and its purpose be clearly portrayed. The Ascension blessing was an empowerment for mission and service, but it was also the promise of Christ to stay "in touch" with the disciples. This aspect of blessing should be obvious for the worshiper from the words used in such a liturgy.

Some Christian traditions have had difficulty in deciding who should articulate the words of God's blessing. The tradition that the apostles were empowered by Christ to dispense the blessing of the exalted Lord has been challenged by those who declare that all Christians through their baptism are part of the corporate priesthood of all believers. However, the issue is not so much who should be allowed to give the blessing as how the worshiper best receives and takes to heart such a blessing. Since the blessing always comes from God, there can be no proper sense in speaking of a bishop's blessing or a priest's blessing. The blessing never belongs to them but to God alone. My experience is that the worshiper best receives the blessing when it is clearly articulated by a person entrusted with this responsibility by the whole Church, and the words they use are those attached to previous memories of blessings received. This experience implies *order* and *continuity*. Such words of blessing truly given will affirm the sense of the empowerment of God and the abiding presence of God in all the circumstances of the worshiper's life.

Unity in worship

At the Ascension the unity of the disciples was cemented by their common loyalty to Jesus as Lord. Luke confirms this unity for us in his record of the Ascension in the opening chapters of the Acts of the Apostles. It is a unity of prayer (Acts 1:14) and a unity of the experience of the Holy Spirit (Acts 2:1, 4). This same unity is experienced by worshipers during the liturgy today. It is a unity in diversity as the worshipers, like the first disciples, recognize that they come from a variety of backgrounds and include both genders (Acts 1:13-14). This experience of our common fellowship in Christ is in marked contrast to the current situation in society as a whole, where the distinctions of gender, age, and culture are stressed.

In their worship the followers of Jesus experience two contrasting features of Christian faith and worship. First we see the Christ and the faith represented *within* our culture, as one of us, belonging to our time and culture. From within our life situation we see the gospel meeting our deepest desires and longings as well as challenging some of our assumptions. On the other hand, we see the Christ as calling us *beyond* our culture into a new universal truth that joins us to all humanity of whatever generation and culture.

Through worship we become very aware of this twofold implication of the doctrine of the Ascension. Christ takes our human experience within the Godhead, and we are taken by the ascended Christ into a new solidarity of being human. We often find it hard to hold these two truths together in unity and balance. We sometimes long to make Christ in our own image, identifying the Christ with our own gender and culture to the exclusion of the "other." We want to domesticate Christ into our pattern of being.

Yet we know that Christ always stretches us through worship to be in touch with all the width and depth of what it means to be human. The young and the old at worship are forced to reach out to one another as they search for the Christ who binds them together. We know that it is never easy to reach harmony in worship in the midst of our diversity. It is only as we become integrated into the ascended Lord that we find we can live fully with and for one another.

The experience of Christians in the ecumenical age of the last fifty years or so is that when they learned to worship together, they found a new unity, which brought delight and challenged them to move closer on the road to unity. The symbol of Church leaders at prayer was always more powerful for unity than a committee negotiating to produce a report. Most ecumenical dialogues have only developed through common worship and prayer. In the presence of Christ at the altar, the offense of separation has been most keenly felt. It was the discovery that worship within the unity of common baptism was right that enabled the members of various Churches to affirm the one journey for the Christian disciple of whatever tradition. The experience of the Ascension and the bestowal of the common gift of the Holy Spirit at Pentecost should allow both aspects of unity and diversity to be acknowledged as treasures bestowed from the divine hand.

The very words we use in worship help us to recognize this diversity and unity. "Amen" is probably the most universal Christian word used in association with prayer. It is accepted in all cultures without translation and yet is identified by each culture as the affirmation of the people at the end of a prayer. Through its use people of every culture can associate themselves with the prayer, even when the language of the prayer itself is a barrier to their involvement. The word "Amen" brings us back to the roots of Christian prayer in the Hebrew language of the first followers of Jesus and of Jesus' own prayers. It is a universal word that concludes a prayer that relates closely to the particular situation, language, and culture of the person uttering the prayer. Taken together the "Amen" and the words of the prayer are a parable of the twin aspects of our unity and diversity in worship.

The bridge between the "then" and the "now"

The doctrine of the Ascension forms a bridge between the Incarnation of Jesus and the eternal nature of Jesus as God. Through liturgical worship we are enabled to keep this bridge open. In worship we recall the life and teaching of the incarnate Christ. The Scriptures tell of this record and form the basic word that is heard in worship. This hearing is amplified through the application of the word to the daily life and witness of the worshipers through their silent meditation and the words of the sermon. Worship, like the Ascension, forms the bridge between the incarnate Word and the contemporary word.

In worship we also place ourselves in the presence of the living, eternal God through our solidarity with the ascended Lord. The focus for the worshiper is not on the memory of the past as an event of long ago but on the past made present through the power of Christ at worship. It is the living Christ who prays with us and for us, giving us strength for our contemporary life and our journey into the future. In the doctrine of the Ascension the Jesus of history becomes the Christ of eternal presence. In worship the "then" and the "now" are so intertwined that they become as one. As the word of Scripture is read, the word of Christ is heard in the context of our current situation. As the bread and wine are offered, the presence of the living Lord is made real. As the blessing is bestowed, the hands of the living Christ are stretched out toward us. As the word of absolution is proclaimed, the saving work of Christ is applied to each penitent. The prominence of the doctrine of the Resurrection has meant that it has often taken within its orbit the aspect of the Ascension. The resurrected Christ is seen as the exalted Christ. Our closer examination has revealed that the doctrine of the Ascension goes beyond that of the Resurrection. It is the Ascension that makes fully clear the bridge between the Incarnation and the Exaltation. This is an important factor for our worship. There we are called to hold together our faith in the reality of the incarnate Christ at the same time as we keep faith with the reality that it is the ascended Christ who holds the responsibility for fulfilling God's purpose for the world and for humanity within it.

Through our worship we are lifted into the heart of God and join our wills to the divine will to work for the coming of the Kingdom. The rule of God as lived out in the incarnate Christ of history is the pattern from which the worshiper seeks guidance, inspiration, encouragement, and empowerment. The Cross becomes a living way of life as the worshiper plumbs the depths of its meaning and applies it to the pain and hope of his or her own life. Through worship we realize that Christ still lives the way of sacrifice and reconciliation. Through worship that which is historical becomes contemporary, and the Jesus of faith is the Christ of our worship.

Distance is overcome by worship

Our final point in applying the doctrine of the Ascension to the principles of worship is an examination of the understanding of distance. The experience of the Ascension shows that distance as associated with Christ's presence can be overcome through worship. The "departure" of Christ at his ascension lifted the disciples into a new experience of the presence of Christ through prayer. What could be thought of as distance became the entrance into presence. The Ascension event allowed the disciples and the current worshiper to access the presence of Christ wherever they were located in time and space.

Even the resurrection appearances allowed Christ to be accessed only by those in certain locations. If Thomas was not with the rest of the disciples when the resurrected Christ appeared, then Thomas had no access to Jesus (John 20:24-29). Thomas had to be in the right location to confront the Christ with his challenge and to respond in faith. After the Ascension, access to Christ was open to any worshiper who drew near in heart and soul. In Christ there was full assurance of access to the Godhead wherever the worshiper might be located.

The expansion of the Church has been built on the principle that Christ and the Godhead can be accessed from any point on the globe and at any time in history. The worshiper is no nearer to Christ in the places of the historical setting of the Jesus of Nazareth. Pilgrimage can enliven faith by making real the geography of the Gospels and assuring the disciple that the gospel is not a fable. We know that the life of Jesus is rooted in geography and in history. Yet the access to the exalted Lord is readily available at whatever time and place suit the worshiper. Christians live by this assumption, but it is important to realize that the assumption rests on the doctrine of the Ascension.

The disciples discovered that the departure of Christ at his Ascension was also the entrance to a new conception of Jesus as the living Lord, fully part of the eternal Godhead and worthy of our praise, adoration, and petition. The doctrine of worship rests on this discovery, and every worshiper is the inheritor of this experience. Because the location of our worship is in heaven, we can be anywhere on earth without any distance between us and Christ. We are already there with Christ and Christ with us.

This understanding of the elimination of distance applies also to Christ's knowledge of our condition. Because of the Ascension, the worshiper is assured that Christ fully understands the human condition in which we find ourselves. We feel no gap between what we describe and the understanding that God has for our situation. We know that the experience of being human is now within the heart of God, and in our worship God empathizes with the reality of the situation in which we find ourselves.

Through worship we are united with the exalted Lord and feel the assurance that no sense of distance can divide us.

Practical implications of these principles for liturgical worship

In Chapter 8 we will examine in more detail some of the practical implications of the principles set out in this chapter. Here in summary it is sufficient to note that the doctrine of the Ascension has clearly shaped the Church's attitude to worship since the days of the first disciples. In looking again at many of the assumptions generally held about worship, we can trace the influence of the doctrine and experience of the Ascension. At various points during this examination we have shown where we think it is important to restore some balance to our current practice of worship so that we can follow more faithfully the essentials of the Ascension doctrine.

CHAPTER 6

The Implications of the Ascension for Our Personal Prayers

The doctrine of the Ascension has major implications for our personal prayers as well as for our corporate liturgies. When we approach the Godhead in prayer, we look for a relationship with the Divine that is personal, moral, loving, growing, and forgiving. Many people are attracted to the person of Jesus Christ as the "window" into the Godhead. Jesus becomes the tangible focus of their relationship with God. The life of Christ becomes their assurance of the nature of the God to whom they pray. All Christians in their prayers want to be certain that the Christ of two thousand years ago is the same as the Christ of our relationship now.

The hinge between the "then" and the "now"

It is the Ascension event that is the hinge between the "then" and the "now." Through the Ascension the Christ, known so well to his contemporaries and described to us in the records of the New Testament, becomes part of the permanence of the Godhead. The Ascension assures us that it is God's purpose to restore the Christ to the eternal existence that belongs to the Divine. The limitations necessary for living in the mortal world of humanity are no longer applicable to the eternal world of the Godhead. We can say too of Christ that "age shall not weary him, nor the years condemn" him to frailty. The "then" and the "now" can be brought together, and the Christ who was the contemporary of the first disciples becomes the same Christ who is our contemporary. The reading of the Gospels is not a search to recover a fading picture of Jesus but a shining illumination into the relationship we can have with Christ now through our prayers.

On the other hand, the departure aspect of the Ascension story emphasizes that physical contact with Jesus is no longer possible or appropriate because it would limit his availability to a particular time, a particular place, and a particular culture. It would fix God back in time, and forever afterward we could only try to look backward at the events of the earthly life of Jesus as if through a telescope. Our prayers, inspired through the Spirit of Christ, allow us the freedom to leave behind the idea that we would know Jesus better if we had lived then and move to the experience of Christ in prayer that connects the "then" and the "now."

The Ascension affirms for us that Christ is fully part of the Godhead. Christ "sits at God's right hand," to use the symbolic language that conveys to us the picture of the truth. Being part of the Godhead, this Christ remains permanently available to us in a mode of existence that we call divine. Therefore we can have instant and ready access to this Christ through our prayers. The time for prayer is always "right"; the location of prayers always brings us close to Christ, and the same Christ is there to listen to our words and understand our thoughts. In essence, we have been taught about the ascended Christ so well that we have grown to assume this kind of availability. It has been at the core of the teaching of Christians about prayer.

Yet we need to remind ourselves from time to time of the basis behind our assumptions. Without upholding the doctrine of the Ascension, we could easily find that the assurance of the presence of Christ becomes merely the assurance of the presence of the Holy Spirit. This is another part of the understanding of prayer, but it does not lead to the same conclusions. Reliance on the doctrine of the Holy Spirit alone removes the element of personal relationship with God through Christ. The moral and human touch is abandoned, and the emphasis on the spiritual presence leaves out the connection with the personal nature of that presence through Christ. For the relationship of prayer to flourish, we need to know that love is rooted in Jesus Christ. We need to realize and experience the challenges of Christ before love degenerates into a feeling of comfort and the cord with the reality of love shown in the historical Christ is snapped. We cannot allow ourselves to be cut off from the vine if the truth about love and relationship is to be maintained.

Human experience within the heart of God

The second implication of the Ascension for our personal prayers arises out of the acknowledgment that the Christ who has fully shared in human experience is the same Christ who prays for us in heaven. Christ has carried what it means to be human right inside the heart of the Godhead. In our cries of joy and pain, which form part of our prayers, we can know that we are not simply heard with sympathy but understood with empathy. That is the point of the passage from the Epistle to the Hebrews (Heb 4:14-16) that we already examined in Chapter 3. When we pour out the longings of the heart in personal prayer, it is vital that we know that such cries are accepted, understood, and responded to by a God who listens to such prayers. There is no doubt from the Gospel record that Jesus listened and responded to such cries from the depth of the hearts of people who approached him. The Gospel writers go to some lengths to let us know that Jesus listened to and responded to "the heart of the matter." Our personal prayers become real as we grasp this reassurance that the ascended Christ knows from the inside what kinds of feelings, hopes, and dreams we have.

It may be true that Christ could not know of the particularities of our own situation as human beings. Each of us is unique; each society has its own culture; each generation has its own technological issues; each gender has its own way of looking at things. Yet the deep cries of the heart arise out of common issues that face humanity. For example, our frustration at the breakdown of communication with other human beings is usually caused by their inability to understand our point of view rather than by the breakdown of the technology of communication. The cell phone has not solved the communication gap between generations—or even between theologians! The Gospel record shows that Jesus understood very well the issues that caused the breakdown of communication between people (and theologians), even if speech and letter-writing were conveyed by different technology.

Diversity is clearly a gift of God's creation and a source of joy to the heart of God. Jesus brought diversity together within a common purpose. The disciples were obviously a diverse group from a variety of backgrounds and with a variety of talents. The early Church was a witness to the glory and the struggle to achieve harmony within diversity. Christ did and does relate to each of us in the commonality of being human, even if not in the particularity of being unique. Our prayer relationship flourishes as we share our common human feelings and experiences with God in Christ, and find hope and strength to accept our humanity even as we move on to reach the goal of life in accordance with the purposes of God.

St. Paul is convinced that in eternity what matters is our unity "in Christ," not the particularity of being Jew or Gentile (that is, our race); male or female (that is, our gender); slave or free (that is, our social position; see Gal 3:28). This unity with Christ and with the community of Christians is equally true in relationship to our prayers if we apply the doctrine of the Ascension to this area of spiritual life.

So Christ shares with us the basic nature of being human and the experiences that go with it. In our personal prayers we can share those experiences with Christ, knowing that we are understood from the inside and that God's strength will equip us to face all the issues that are common to humanity.

Responsibility for the fulfillment of redemptive love

The third implication of the Ascension for our personal prayers is that we know from the position of the ascended Christ that God has given Christ responsibility within the Godhead for the fulfillment of the purposes of God. Christ is set at God's right hand. All authority, dominion, and power has been given to him so that the purpose of the creation can be brought to full fruition. This means that the life and teaching of the incarnate Christ are at one with the intentions of the Godhead. What Christ shows us as the purposes of God while on earth was not a temporary arrangement to suit the particular conditions Jesus faced but was in accordance with the permanent principles on which God's world existed—then and now. So Christ's teaching that redemptive love is at the very heart of the purposes of God holds equally true for our generation as it did for the first generation of God's people. The initiative behind Christ's Incarnation was to bring back the lost within the orbit of God's will and purpose. They were to be brought back to be part of the community that would effect justice, righteousness, and peace.

Within the Godhead, Christ continues to work to make this redemptive love effective in the lives of people of every generation. God's will is to be done through love. That "the Lamb is in the midst of the throne" (Rev 7:17) signifies that the redemptive, sacrificial love shown on the cross is at the very heart of the rule of God. This has a personal significance for us in our prayers. It means that we can approach God to find renewal and forgiveness and can expect to be greeted with affection and seriousness. God will delight in our recognition that we need forgiveness and a change of heart, and we can be sure that God will free us from the guilt that would otherwise cripple the progress in our relationship with God. We will not hide our sins from such a God but pour them out of a troubled heart to find the balm of absolution.

We are often held back from approaching God for forgiveness because we are afraid that we will be met with cold judgment, with condemnation and a declaration of worthlessness. We are afraid that we will be cut off and thrown into the fires of hell. We see God as Judge and do not believe that the loving, tender Christ has any power in the decisions of judgment. Proper reflection will see that this attitude divides the Trinity and is a confusion of good theology, but it is often the way we feel at the time in the midst of guilt and shame. Our human experiences of seeking forgiveness from "authority figures" and the way that we have been met with condemnation may reinforce such feelings. So the doctrine that the ascended Christ is in the position of responsibility encourages us in our personal prayers to seek forgiveness. The purpose of the Cross is our salvation, not our condemnation, for the Lamb is in the midst of the throne.

Once we have experienced this forgiveness, we will want to add our weight to the principle of redemptive love. We will desire with all our heart to forgive others and to proclaim that redemptive love is at the center of the purposes of God. We will know that the power that lies at the heart of God is the power of love to bring about the healing of the world, in the lives of individuals and in the life of society. In the end this healing of humanity will result in the restoration of the whole of creation. The "shalom" of God—the peace, unity, and wholeness of all things in their proper relationship to God and one another—will be the outcome of the work of the ascended Christ.

Partnership with the prayers of the ascended Christ

The method that Jesus Christ used to apply this redemptive love to the needs of the world was to draw human beings into partnership with him. He did not carry out his ministry on his own. Instead, he consciously drew others into the plans and the purposes of God. He called them into a partnership in which all would work to build up the "body," Christ's presence and power among people. To some degree, God constantly refuses to act without us, even though by the nature of God this is always an active possibility. Mary's "yes" was part of the Incarnation without limiting the power of God both to take the initiative and to work without us if that proves a necessity to achieve the overall purposes of God.

Through our personal prayers the ascended Christ calls us into partnership in working for the fulfillment of the purposes of God. It is through prayer that we enter into the heart and mind of God. We reestablish our priorities and see ourselves and our fellow human beings in a new light—as God sees us. Through prayer we recognize our part in the Kingdom of God and receive the power to do those things that are required of us in such a partnership.

The teaching of the incarnate Christ about prayer is clear from the Gospel record. Prayer was an activity to which all disciples were called. Jesus gave his disciples and us the pattern for all our praying. In our prayers the following themes are to be obvious:

- our relationship with God;
- our worship and respect of God;

- our dedication to the purposes of God;
- our acceptance of forgiveness from God;
- our readiness to forgive others;
- our acknowledgment that power belongs to God alone;
- our assurance of the permanence of God.

Because of the Ascension we can be sure that Christ still calls us to be disciples at prayer. Such prayer is the work of intercession for the fulfillment of the purposes of God as well as the work of growth in our own relationship with God. We have the privilege as well as the duty to be involved in releasing the spiritual energy required to create a world of harmony and goodness. We are not passive spectators of what God does in the world but active participants in the work of furthering the Kingdom of God. We pray for justice and peace to add our spiritual strength to those who with us seek for righteousness. We pray for strength, guidance, and supporting grace for those who make key decisions on behalf of us all. We pray for consolation and care for those who suffer in any way. We pray for wisdom, knowledge, and discernment for those who pursue the discovery of truth.

In this work of prayer we join the ascended Christ, who is constantly making intercession for us and for the whole world (see Heb 7:25). We are called to live in union with Christ through our baptism, and so we are part of his praying activity, which gives to our created order the spiritual energy necessary to fulfill the purposes of the Creator. God *chooses to seek our partnership* in this work, and when we respond we are part of the team that prays individually and corporately.

Our intercessions also contribute significantly to the building up of the relationship between ourselves and God. Our intercessions often reveal our priorities and the deepest desires of our hearts. These prayers declare what is important for us. As we apply our understanding of Scripture to our prayers, we sometimes find that we are challenged to reorder our priorities. In prayer we open ourselves up to listen to what God wants as well as to what we think we want. This leads to the dialogue with God that shapes our dreams, directs our energies, and brings us closer to the heart of God.

Our Amen to the prayer of Christ

The understanding of the work of the ascended Christ at prayer has practical outcomes for our work of intercession. Some Christians feel overburdened with the responsibility of being a partner in prayer. They lengthen their intercession list to try to see that all are included. They become worried that the sick will remain unhealed because of the lack of intensity in the faith of the intercessor. They fear that their unrepented sin is hindering the process for peace throughout the world.

The Ascension doctrine helps us to see our part in the partnership of prayer in perspective. In our prayers we are heavenbound, sharing in the doing of God's will and adding our energy for the achievement of God's purpose. By praying "with Christ," we are uttering our human Amen—may this prayer come true and be true—to Christ's prayer of loving redemption, re-creation and restoration, wholeness and healing, peace and unity, both for individuals in their struggles and for collective groups of people in their growth to maturity. Once we grasp this truth we know that our prayer does not suffer from being too weak but gains strength as it adds weight to the whole prayer. Because it is Christ's prayer and we affirm it with our Amen, we are only called to add the signature of faith to make the prayer more effective for the work of redemptive love. Yet the affirmation of faith through the Amen is necessary. The generosity and grace of God must be received to make them effective in our lives and in the lives of others. Our Amen—your will be done—is an offering of human love in response to the divine love and models for others what they can do to make God's grace effective in their lives. Every Amen is a joy to the God who graciously awaits human cooperation and partnership.

The Amen of humanity is the voice not only of individuals but of the whole body of Christ, that is, the Christian community. As we realize the importance of humanity's Amen to affirm Christ's prayer, so we become aware that our individual Amen is part of the total and corporate Amen of all the faithful. Our intercessions may be made by us as individuals, but they flow as part of the river of the Church's prayers. That does not make our intercessions any less important, but it does make us aware of the corporate strength behind the work of intercession. Our small Amens combine to create the loud Amen of the whole people of God. This gives us encouragement in our prayers of intercession and takes away the anxiety of failure, which is rooted in pride. We can no longer think that it was our prayers that created the miracle but God's grace affirmed by the Amen of all people.

The use of symbol as an aid to prayer

The description of the Ascension event and the symbolic language used in the Scriptures in reference to the ascended Christ can help us to see the value of symbol and pictures in our times of prayer. Too often prayer is seen as an activity of the lips; it becomes restricted to the expression of words. The Ascension helps us to see how limited such a view is. Symbols and pictures can be an important source of inspiration in prayer. Within the Orthodox tradition, icon and prayer are so closely intertwined that the icon can be the means by which we pray. In the Spirit we can find in the icon the unity between ourselves and God—a unity of heart and mind, of will and purpose. Symbols such as a cross, a flower, or a candle can bring us into the presence of the ascended Christ, there to join our wills to God's will, which is at the heart of prayer.

The Ascension doctrine helps us to see that the limitations of logic should not be used to restrict the perception of the truth. Other parts of our being can respond to God as well as our minds. We have the inner eye of faith, which can just as often use pictures to experience God. There is biblical support for such an approach. The parables of Christ reveal the truth through the pictures they create in our mind from the story that is told. We grasp the truth intuitively rather than logically.

In our prayers it is important that we affirm this principle that comes from an understanding of the Ascension story. We can pray for someone by holding them in our mind's eye to receive the touch of blessing from God. Words formulated into a prayer are not always necessary in such a case. We may prefer to utter a single Amen at the end of the time of prayer. The picture becomes our way of praying.

Symbols will also help us to connect the historical Christ with the contemporary Christ of faith and experience. In our Christmas adoration we may find that we wish to kneel before the manger as we gaze in faith on God Emmanuel. A crib scene may be used in our home as part of the decorations for the festival. Year by year it will connect us not only to the first Christmas but to our past celebrations of the festival. It will bring forward for us all the memories of the experiences of God in wonder, joy, and even pain. It will "pick up" our past prayers and renew our relationship with God through prayer. Likewise, the cross of Calvary, the Easter light, the fire of Pentecost will all encourage times of reflection and intercession. Our symbols become our windows into heaven, just as the Ascension was the window into heaven for the first disciples.

Some Christians find it helpful to light a candle in a holy space as a symbol of their prayer. Logic says that there is little use in such a practice, but insight says that the candle can speak firmly of our intention. It is like a sacrament for us. It is a visible sign of our prayer, which otherwise remains an invisible reality. In a theological sense, we can make a parallel comment about the Ascension event. This was the visible sign of the invisible reality that Christ was now to be experienced in spiritual rather than physical terms.

We will also have our own symbols, which are personal to us because of the memories of God that they hold. These may range from a picture to a printed Scripture verse, from a souvenir from a pilgrimage to a palm cross kept from a previous Holy Week service. The value is in the memories of God that they invoke and the inspiration they give to our prayers. Symbols should never restrict our experience of God but should draw us into a renewed presence of the God who ever relates to us in our times of prayer. Here again there is a parallel with the Ascension, which opened the door to future experiences of Christ for the first disciples.

Anticipation of the union with Christ in heaven

This leads us to the final implication of the Ascension for our personal prayers. The experience of the Ascension, like the Transfiguration, opened the eyes of the disciples to the true nature of this Jesus. It drew them on in their hope of a final experience of union with Christ in heaven. This understanding of the Ascension helps us at prayer to see that as we join Christ with our Amen to the will of God, we gain a foretaste of our eternity. We come to understand the satisfaction that comes from being part of the purpose and will of God. Our longings move toward fulfillment. We come to see the place we have in God's Kingdom. We realize again our value and worth to God as we work in partnership with the divine will.

Prayer becomes for us an activity in which the soul rejoices in the exercise of its proper role. It lifts us from looking inward into ourselves and turns us outward to take our part in the fulfillment of the Creator's design. Prayer gives us that sense of completion of our being that finds its home with God. We know in prayer that we are doing what we were created to do: to join God in bringing the whole world into harmony.

Such prayer is at the same time both a denial of self and a fulfillment of self. It is a denial of self because we must let go of the futility of thinking that we would be happy if only our individual needs and concerns were met. We have to let go of the self as the center of all things, with its desires to be pampered and pleased. Pleasing self never proves to be satisfying because, as we reach the goal we had set, it turns out to be worthless. We have to turn our back on our plans so that we can find true pleasure in the goal set for us: union with God through Christ.

The Cross teaches us to accept with gladness our role in redemptive love and to offer a sacrifice of our Amen to the work of Christ. Though our sacrifice cannot be compared to that of Christ on Calvary, in prayer we find that God affirms our offering as important for the life of the world. Such affirmation brings us ever closer to the ascended Christ at prayer. We discover joy in our unity with Christ.

The Ascension helps us to see that in this earthly life we can gaze upward with wonder but cannot join Christ in the physical sense. The departure must be accepted before the presence of Christ in the new reality of spiritual prayer can be understood. This union with Christ is a joy, but yet we know that it cannot be compared to the glory that is yet to be for us. Our prayers are indeed

a foretaste of the heavenly banquet and as such give us both satisfaction and hope. The closer we become to the ascended Christ in
prayer, the more we long for the union of heaven itself. Then we
will fully know what we should be praying for and how we can
best fulfill our role as partners in union with Christ.

As the Ascension is the prelude to the gift of the Holy Spirit,
so our prayer with the ascended Christ is inspired by that same
Spirit. Through the spiritual experience of prayer we become
Spirit-filled and have the means by which to unite more fully with
Christ. With hearts lifted to heaven in prayer, we grow toward that
for which we pray: a full relationship with our Creator God
through the prayer of Christ and the breath of the Spirit, which
quickens us to eternal life.

Summary

In this chapter we have seen how the understanding of the
doctrine and event of the Ascension has a dramatic impact on our
life of prayer, giving us encouragement and direction. It has
helped us to discard over-reliance on logic and to put proper emphasis on intuition and insight in our prayer life. We have seen the
reasons why we should add our Amen to the prayer of Christ and
look forward in hope to the fuller unity of spirit with Christ in our
"last days."

CHAPTER 7

The Implications of the Doctrine of the Ascension for Preaching

Because the feast of the Ascension falls each year on a Thursday in the ten days before Pentecost, few members of the congregation hear a sermon on its meaning and its implications for their Christian lives. The calendar provides for a Sunday after Ascension, but this can often be used by the preacher to highlight the need to be prepared for Pentecost, the third great festival in the Christian year. The few who attend on Ascension Day itself are often embarrassed by the preacher's apologies about the difficulty of the account and the lack of consistency about the event in the biblical record. For the preacher, the opportunity to give a sermon for Ascension is not always seen as a positive one, although the associated issues of the Great Commission, Christ at prayer, and the end of the Resurrection appearances can provide a good lead.

Too often the Church overlooks the feast of the Ascension altogether or relegates it to a Eucharist or evening service without the need for a sermon. Such an action is both unnecessary and unwise. The doctrine of the Ascension has much to say to the worshiper, as we have discovered in the preceding chapters. We are now aware that the doctrine forms part of the Creeds, and for this reason we must consider it an essential part of the doctrine of the Christian Church. It is therefore the duty of those appointed as preachers for the feast to use the opportunity to the full. They can enlighten the congregation on the importance of the implications of the doctrine and the assistance that it gives to the fulfillment of many of the responsibilities that they undertake as Christians.

In this chapter I aim to provide material that will help the preacher undertake the task gladly and gain the reward that good preaching brings. I have appended two examples of sermons that I have actually preached on the feast so that preachers can judge for themselves how effective my thoughts have been in practice. They must be used as examples only and not be preached again, because the congregation and the context are never the same on a later occasion.

First let me set out what I consider the tasks of a preacher to be on all occasions when they are asked to provide the sermon. They can be summarized as follows:

- To relate the passage of Scripture to the experience of this particular people of God listening to the Word on this particular day.
- To examine the context of the chosen passage of Scripture so that the people can see how it relates to the total life, ministry, and teaching of Jesus Christ.
- To relate the passage of Scripture to the doctrine of the Church and the understanding of contemporary theology.
- To allow the people to gain access to the symbolism and story contained in the passage and to use it as a spring board for their worship and witness.
- To encourage the people to be aware of and fulfill their responsibilities as Christians.
- To help the people stay in touch with the realities of human life in themselves and in others.
- To free the people to use their emotions as a way of entering into the presence of God.
- To help the people to reach ethical decisions for themselves and their communities that are in conformity with the Christian understanding of human relationships.

All these tasks the preacher has to carry out using the best methods of communication available on that particular occasion. The spoken word can be enhanced by all the modern aids to communication. However, it is vital that a sermon always has the element of personal witness and a person-to-person encounter. This fulfills the doctrine of the Incarnation—the Word made flesh.

The doctrine of the Ascension is able to help the preacher fulfill these tasks. I look at each task in turn and provide some notes as to how we can use the Ascension to make the necessary connections for the people.

1. The Ascension is about the human experience of the divine. The biblical passages that we examined in Chapter 3 all tell how Jesus Christ relates to his disciples or to the tasks that the ascended Christ now does for the welfare of all disciples. All of us understand well the dynamics of departure. We are familiar with farewells. We know what it feels like to say goodbye; we have had to find the words to take our leave of another person. The Ascension is therefore part of our human experience if only we are helped to see it in that light. It is quite easy for the preacher, therefore, to make the connections and gain the attention of the people for the sermon.

2. We have now seen that the Ascension is an essential element in the life of Christ—while on earth as well as now in heaven. It is in line with the teaching of Christ that he would not leave the disciples bereft without a new, if different, way of being in touch with him. The Ascension marks the conclusion of the Incarnation, so that the worshiper can hold together the Jesus of history and the Christ of faith. The Ascension helps us come to grips with the question as to what activity Christ is carrying out for us now. Without the Ascension the Incarnation is left "up in the air." Scripture does not portray Jesus as having just disappeared from the scene, nor does it encourage us to hang around the shores of Lake Galilee or the city of Jerusalem in the hope of a repeat resurrection experience. The preacher needs to use the Ascension to affirm this witness. The Ascension marks the clear conclusion of experiencing Jesus Christ in one mode and points to the way we can experience the same Jesus in the proper mode for today.

3. The preacher can use the Ascension to highlight the many doctrines of the Church. It can help the people of God understand the meaning of Christ as King and the reign of God; what constitutes heaven; the way the Holy Spirit is the Spirit of the risen Lord; prayer and the work of intercession; the end times and their foretaste now; and of course the Incarnation and Resurrection as a permanent principle in the life of Christ and not just a temporary

arrangement. The Ascension doctrine can be used by the preacher from year to year to relate to all these issues and to give the congregation a clear grasp of the doctrines of the Church.

4. The feast of the Ascension can provide the preacher with an opportunity to highlight the use of symbolism in the Bible and in worship. The preacher is not required to explain symbolism so much as to explore it. The use of symbolism is important for us because we experience God not only through words and logic but through symbolism and intuition. It is important in an age that is still dominated by the value placed on logic and "scientific" fact to stress the value of symbol. Fortunately most Christians are aware that God is accessed through symbol and story, sacrament and senses. The sacraments of baptism and Holy Communion speak strongly to them as avenues by which they can be in touch with the power and love of God. These two sacraments are dominated by symbol, memory, and experience. The clouds of the Ascension story can be explored by the preacher as the way the disciples can "see" the presence and power of God at work. Through such symbolism the preacher can also connect one Scripture passage to others and thus help the people of God gain greater insights into the Bible as a whole.

5. Sermons are not occasions for lectures from the preacher to the people about morals. Yet it is important that the preacher encourage the people to identify their responsibilities to others and to put them into practice in accordance with each individual situation. Too often the duties of a Christian are reduced to the dictum: "Do unto others as you would wish them to do unto you." This is not a sufficient principle for Christian behavior. It is far too narrow and far too selfish. The Ascension doctrine allows the preacher to look at a much wider range of Christian responsibilities. These would include prayer, affirmation, adoration, mission, mutual care, care of self, encouragement, respect for all humanity, the use of the gifts of the Spirit, and the promotion of cultural diversity.

6. The Ascension allows the preacher to expound the reality of being human as it tells how the ascended Christ takes the experience of that condition into the Godhead. For the people this will raise the issue of saying that we are one with all humanity, knowing that we are all in many ways different from one another and

unique. When we recognize that the humanity of Christ is permanently an experience of the Godhead, we have to come to terms with the issues of human suffering, human sexuality, and human diversity. The Ascension allows the acknowledgment of the diversity of gender and culture without denying the common bonds of humanity. Because of the Ascension doctrine, we know that we can fully share our joys and tribulations with Christ in prayer, in the faith that Christ understands them from the inside of the experience. In this way the preacher has many opportunities in the sermon to keep the people in touch with the reality of human life.

7. The feast of the Ascension is a timely occasion for the preacher to encourage the people to use their emotions to feel that they are close to Christ. Many people seem to feel that Christ is now far distant from them as worshipers, because Scripture says that he has gone far from his disciples, never to be seen again. Our study has shown that the Ascension was the bridge for the first disciples to link their feeling of sorrow at the parting of Christ with their new experience of the presence of the Spirit of Christ. The feast is an opportunity to help the people to claim who Christ is for them and how they can be aware of being empowered and blessed for their task of mission in the world.

8. All Christians have strong memories of the words in the Lord's Prayer and especially of the line "your kingdom come, your will be done." All wrestle with the task of trying to decide what the will of God is in any given situation. The Ascension helps the preacher to share with the people the permanent principle that the will of God is to bring redemptive love into action in every situation. The preacher can encourage the people to work out the details of this principle and to assure them that the ascended Christ is at prayer for them to give them courage and strength. The preacher will know of practical examples in the life of the congregation to show how to do the will of God through love of neighbor and of self.

In these ways the preacher will use the Ascension doctrine as a springboard by which the congregation can apply the Scripture reading to their own lives, and then in prayer seek strength from God to exercise their responsibilities. I believe that preachers, once they have made the connections for themselves, will eagerly seize the opportunities that a sermon at Ascensiontide can provide to fulfill their tasks. Since their congregations are well aware that the doctrine of the Church as set forth in the Creeds includes the Ascension and that the event is recorded in Luke's Gospel and in Acts, but that there is confusion about the doctrine among many clergy and laity, any help that the preacher can give to them will be welcomed with open arms. The reward I have found from preaching at Ascension has been to see the look of delight and relief on the faces of the congregation and receive their words of sincere thanks.

To complete this chapter, I now include the promised two examples of sermons preached on the feast of the Ascension. The first focuses on the place of heaven in the mind of people and the way our understanding of heaven is enlightened by the doctrine of the Ascension. The second applies the doctrine of the Ascension to the nature of being human. Other topics that have been the subject of sermons at Ascensiontide have been the nature of prayer, the work of intercession, and the theology of religious art.

A SERMON FOR ASCENSIONTIDE

Our citizenship is in heaven

It is not very fashionable to talk about heaven these days. Our focus is on our troubled earth and our day-to-day existence. In celebrating the festivals, many more people attend church at Christmas than they do at Ascensiontide.

Yet the teaching of the New Testament on the Ascension is that the Incarnation of Christ is completed by the Ascension of Christ. Then he takes his place "in the heavens." This is an expression meaning the place where the fullness of God dwells. In our baptism Christians become one with Christ and dwell in him. In this way we, too, have our citizenship in heaven. To be a citizen is to have rights and also responsibilities in that community.

In our time of reflection this morning, I want to lead your thoughts to answer these questions:

What does heaven mean for us?
What are our rights or benefits as citizens of heaven?
And what are our responsibilities?

Heaven is a place where we experience the presence of God in its fullness. It is not only a future hope but a current reality. We can enjoy the presence of God in our lives now as well as in our resurrection. When Christ ascended and the disciples witnessed his withdrawal from his bodily form on earth, they experienced most of all Christ's blessing.

To be blessed is to be made whole, to know that we are valued, that we are part of God's purpose, and to be filled with the peace and joy of God. One of the continuing tasks of priests and bishops in the Church is to make this blessing of God constantly available to Christians and to those who will receive it. When we are blessed we know that we are one with God in mutual love and adoration and that we are empowered in our deepest being. To be blessed is to experience well-being at its deepest level. We are "in touch with the divine"—and that's heaven.

Heaven is a place of prayerful activity. The ascended Christ is pictured in the epistles of the New Testament as constantly praying for the world. Christ by his ascension has not withdrawn from involvement in our experiences, but he has discarded the limitations of human existence. "In heaven" Christ can be everywhere at once, available to all who seek him in prayer. Christ should be seen as carrying us in his prayerful heart, and not only us but all the world. I saw a lovely illustration of this in a stained-glass window in the large church built for worship by the Taizé community in central France. Down one side aisle facing the sun is a set of small windows, each portraying one of the key events in the life of Christ: his Incarnation, his baptism, his entry into Jerusalem, his crucifixion, his Resurrection, his Ascension, and his final return in glory.

In the Ascension window the artist shows the Christ seated in heaven. He is dressed in deepest sky blue, and to his heart he holds a bright yellow globe of the world. Christ's prayer enfolds the world in the heart of God through sacrificial love. In our intercessions we join Christ in this action, enfolding those who need empowerment, healing, peace, and strength into the heart of God.

Heaven is the place of obedience. In the Lord's Prayer we pray: "Your kingdom come, your will be done, on earth as it is in heaven." Heaven is the place where God's will is done and God's law reigns. We join Christ not only in prayer but in full obedience, right thinking and doing. When we are obedient to God, we have to stand apart from many of our fellow citizens on earth. They obey a different law, seeking first their own good and advancement, through greed and violence if necessary. The conditions we find in our community should not surprise us even if they shock us. Few of our neighbors think or act as Christians. Their minds are not on the same track as ours, so how could they possibly be expected to arrive at the same destination? Christ gave us the directions for our journey in life, and only by following them can we reach the destination of heaven.

Heaven is the place of worship. Every time we gather for worship, we enjoy the presence of God and offer God our adoration and praise. To be at worship is to enjoy a whole new dimension in our life. It refocuses our being in tune with God. It puts us in harmony with the divine. The God who creates and sustains our universe knows its purpose and empowers it. To join God in worship is somehow to feel part of the total harmony of being and purpose that is divine. There is no higher task and no greater joy.

The Ascension of Christ lifted us all into a new dimension of worship. We could experience Christ as one with us, yet from the heart of God. The earthly limitations of time, place, and generation were no longer relevant for the worshiper. I do not have to go backward in *time* to meet Christ or *travel* to a small country with places like Bethlehem, Jerusalem, or Galilee to worship Christ. I do not have to become a Jew to be one with him in *race* in order to worship and be understood by him. As I lift my heart to heaven, I can find the Christ who is already my brother and my neighbor. When I traveled the continents last year, I found that each congregation identified Christ as one who was one with them and yet transcended them as one with all humanity. Heaven has that quality. There we can worship in our own language and at the same time become caught up in the multitude of tongues.

What rights do we have as citizens of heaven? First, we have the right to be ourselves at our very best. In heaven we not only value God, but in turn we are valued by God. Because Christ has experienced what it means to live with the limitations of our human existence, God understands our cries of ecstasy and confusion, our cries of pain, and our pleas for forgiveness. God not only understands us as Creator but, from the experience of Christ, as our Brother. We have a right in heaven to tell it as it is to God in total honesty and to know that we will be understood and encouraged.

Second, we have a right to expect and to receive empowerment to carry out the tasks of being a Christian in the world. The feast of the Ascension is the prelude to Pentecost—that witness to the faithfulness of God's promise to give the disciples power from on high to witness and serve in the world. As the record of the Acts of the Apostles shows, the trust that Christ had in his disciples was fulfilled as they spread his message of hope, peace, forgiveness, and joy throughout the world. You and I are still writing the next chapter of the Acts of the Apostles in our day and generation.

Third, our right is to have the expectation that what we begin now will be continued in our resurrection to its ultimate perfection. This sense of continuity between our existence now and in eternity is a wonderful comfort for Christians. We will experience change, but there will be vital aspects of being that continue. The doctrine of the Ascension helps us to understand this change and continuity. At the Ascension the disciples experienced the withdrawal of the bodily form of Christ, and yet he continued to be with them in a spiritual form that would go before them on any journey. Christ had left them, but he also left them his promise to be with them always to the end of time.

What then are our responsibilities as citizens of heaven? We must be people who obey the rules of heaven—how to worship, how to live in relation with God and with our neighbor. We will not enjoy our place in the community of God if we constantly want to go our own way. There is no way that we can control the place to suit our own purposes. That would be chaotic for all. We must live as God chooses, not as we decide. Our generation has been falsely told that human beings can be in control of everything. There are those who want to organize their birth, their death, and everything in between. That is not the way we can live in heaven; for our world is not designed for individuals but for community, working out God's plan.

Our second responsibility is to join Christ at prayer. Our intercessions release the divine energy in others if they are ready to allow that to happen. All our services of worship leave space for the essential activity of intercessory prayer. Remember, we join Christ; we do not have to carry the full weight ourselves.

Our third responsibility is to be united with all the other citizens of heaven. Our citizenship allows us to belong to the United Nations at worship. We cannot claim individual, racial, or gender superiority. To be citizens is to find our place in a very diverse community, but one united in the joy and purpose of God. In heaven unity and diversity are two aspects of the same experience.

Thus the Ascension is a key event in the life of Christ, and we note it with wonder and love. Christ has begun the journey to heaven before us and calls us to follow until we too know what it means to be citizens of heaven and fellow citizens with all the saints.

ANOTHER SERMON FOR ASCENSIONTIDE

Common humanity within the heart of God

This Sunday we prepare for the feast of the Ascension, which we celebrate next Thursday. This feast has not received much attention in the Church for a number of years. The reasons for this are both practical (it always falls on a Thursday and is jammed in between the high points of Easter and Pentecost) and doctrinal (most people think of Jesus as being raised into heaven at Easter). Therefore we are left without time or cause for the Ascension.

This is a great pity, because the Ascension has points to teach us about God that are equal in importance to those connected to Easter and Pentecost. I preached about the Ascension in this church a few years ago, so I will not repeat the full range of points, but today I will focus on *one* key aspect of the doctrine.

Jesus' continuity of experience

The Ascension helps us to understand that there is a continuity of experience between the Jesus who lived, died, and rose again as a human being and the exalted Christ who from the Ascension onward takes his place again within the Godhead—the Father, the Son, and the Holy Spirit—as part of the relationship between the Creator, the Redeemer, and the Life-giver. To put it another way, the Christ who sits at the place of responsibility in heaven is the same Christ who shared our human nature with its joys and pain, its empathy and understanding for all things human. The Ascension is the lifting up of humanity within the heart of God. Therefore, the Ascension opens for us the way to heaven as Jesus promised in today's gospel.

You will remember from the Bible readings on the Sundays since Easter that the resurrected Christ gave his disciples signs of this continuity. The hands and the side he showed them were marked with the wounds of the nails and the sword. The Jesus who was crucified was the same Jesus who was raised from death in the tomb. The Jesus who walked in Galilee and shared meals at the lakeside was the same Jesus who knew the familiar spots on the beach where he made his resurrection appearances. The Jesus who broke the bread in the Upper Room in Jerusalem was the same Jesus who made himself known to the two disciples at their home in Emmaus as he broke the bread. Jesus spoke the same words of peace as he greeted his friends both before and after his death and resurrection. There was indeed a continuity. Yet we may liken this to the feeling of continuing presence that many people have shortly after a loved person has died. The issue for the disciples and for us was whether this continuity would come to an end as the months passed.

What the experience of the Ascension did was to show the disciples that this continuity within the human experience was taken permanently into the heart and being of the eternal Godhead. The Ascension showed that the Incarnation—the sharing of humanity through Jesus—was not a passing phase in God's experience. Its essence became a permanent feature of the Godhead.

Does God still know what it is like to be human?

After the Ascension the disciples could find an answer to the obvious questions that they and we want to put to God:

Do you understand what it is like to be human?
Have you ever faced opposition to justice and truth?
Have you ever struggled to decide between choices?
Have you ever shed tears at the death of a loved one?
Have you ever been persecuted for your faith in God?
Have you ever been driven from your home as a refugee?
Do you know what it is like to grow up as a teenager?
Have you ever lost a parent by death?
Have you known the joy of sharing with a circle of friends?
Have you faced the prospect of death?
Have you been through the process of suffering and death?
Have you experienced resurrection to eternal life?

Because of the Ascension we can with confidence and faith respond to each of these questions with a certain "yes." God does know what it means to share fully in the human experience, and Jesus has carried that experience into the heart of God, where it remains permanently. God understands what it means to be human not only from the outside but from the inside; and it goes on being God's experience continually, from the inside.

That affirmation raises a really vital question about the nature of humanity as well as about the nature of God.

Uniquely human

Each human being is said to be unique. We belong to a particular time and place, to our own gender and generation, to our own race and culture. The DNA and the fingerprint make us distinct—special with a clear distinction! In the light of this perception of what it means to be human, the modern person asks this searching question: If each person is unique, how can you say that Jesus understands what it means to be human? As the current fashionable thinking marks out each one of us as distinctive, in the hope that we will therefore be distinguished, with innate superiority we divide humanity up

- into age groups—senior citizens to cradle children;
- into gender—male on this side and female on that;

- into races—Chinese, European, Maori, Asian, Polynesian, African;
- into cultures—Pakeha, Irish, French, Maori, even West Coast;
- into intelligence groups—bright, basic, slow, brilliant.

As we divide humanity into groups, we find fewer and fewer people in our group, until we are alone: there is no one just like us; no one we can fully relate to; no one who can understand us in depth. So we are stuck in our isolation. That seems to be the current way of thinking.

God's correction

The Ascension doctrine helps us to see that such an attitude is madness and a heresy. It is madness because in isolation, starved of love, we will go crazy. It is a heresy because God created humanity for community without division of age, gender, race, or culture. God created humanity for a relationship—with God and with all other people.

I believe that the modern thinking about human nature is also dangerous. It leads to the break-up of community, to jealousy between the genders and the generations, and ultimately to ethnic cleansing and apartheid.

The truth is that God created us with much more that is common about our humanity than is distinctive within humanity. We all breathe the same air; we all share the range of human emotions of fear and happiness; we all long for relationships of love and care; we all seek to reach out to the Divine. We must be humble enough to own up to the fact that we are human, just as a tree is a tree. Trees come in a variety of colors, shapes, and sizes, and so do humans!

Common humanity

It was Archbishop Desmond Tutu who taught me the difference between the essentials of common humanity and the accidents of our distinctions from one another. No one, he told us, says that you are different just because some people have blue eyes and some have gray, green, or brown eyes. The color of our eyes in this sense is an accident of birth. Archbishop Tutu went on to ask: "If we don't make much of the distinction between the color of our eyes, why do we make such a fuss about the color of our skin?" A very good question indeed, which makes us rethink our whole attitude to being part of common humanity.

Jesus our true brother

In the light of such rethinking, the Ascension doctrine shows us that we can truly claim Jesus as our brother in common humanity, sharing all that is essential to the human condition and making it part of the ongoing experience of God. And if Jesus is our brother in humanity, so is every other human being. We belong to God and to one another. That is the truth, and we forget it at our peril. It is one of the glorious truths of the Ascension for which I say:

Thanks be to God!

CHAPTER 8

The Implications of the Doctrine of the Ascension for Future Liturgical Practice

In this chapter we will look at questions that arise for us in regard to how far it is right to picture Christ as "one of us" in our worship without losing sight of the Christ of history. These questions will take us into issues concerning the importance of culture and gender in future liturgical writing, and the search, in recent times, to create specific liturgies appropriate to the particular culture, age, and gender of the worshipers.

In examining liturgical art, it is obvious that the artists do not attempt to portray the historical Christ in any detail but use symbol to maintain the connection between the imagined and the historical scene. In relation to this, questions arise as to the "proper" culture and gender in which to portray the person of Christ. Is the symbol of a man for Christ essential for theological truth, or can an artist show a female figure or a human being of non-specific gender to be an inclusive representation of the Christ? These are some of the questions that face us for the future as a result of this study.

A local or a universal liturgy?

From the evidence available, it would seem that in the worship of the early Church certain embedded words were retained in a liturgy even when new liturgies were composed in the various languages of the newly founded churches. Examples of such words still known to us today are *Amen, Maranatha,* and *Alleluia.* These were probably key words said by the people, and they were handed on in the original language of Christ's usage. The use of such words would remind the people of the connection with Christ himself and would also be a strong link between Christians of different language groups. The widespread usage of Koine Greek in the first-century world also enabled a common liturgy and the Scriptures to be used by people of many different cultures. The writings in the New Testament follow this form of the Greek language. In the liturgy the Aramaic and Hebrew tongues were probably used by those of that culture, including the Church in Jerusalem under James and by some Christian converts from the Jews of the Dispersion. The evidence of the speeches in the Acts of the Apostles and of the Pauline epistles show that those who spread the gospel were always ready to adopt the language of the culture of the people to whom they went.

The evidence of the first recorded liturgies whose texts have been handed on to us is that the presider had a substantial amount of freedom to phrase the Great Thanksgiving Prayer within his own context. We do not know whether this means that a variety of languages were used, but this is at least a possibility. I have no doubt that the key factor in such consideration was that the people at worship should understand the words of the liturgy. The concept of a set form of words for the great prayers of the Church seems to have developed later. Then there was need to guard against heretical teaching as liturgies reflected the views of those who held different interpretations of doctrine. These same issues face the Church today as the new millennium begins. Liturgy always reflects doctrines held, and each language may express doctrine in a slightly different form.

Some problems in translating liturgy

Difficulties arise in translating key theological ideas into a new language in which there is no obvious equivalent in the new tongue. The translator at this point is faced with two main possibilities. Either the original word can be retained and the meaning of that word learned by those at worship, or the nearest equivalent in the new language can be employed. In the latter case, some of the previous ideas associated with that new word will color the theological concept that the author wants to convey.

We can use the example of the word *heaven*. As we saw in the previous section, heaven is an idea with many shades of meaning. It is the place of God's existence and the expression of God's rule and kingdom. Many cultures have an idea that God dwells in the upper reaches of the sky, maybe even "above the clouds." If the translator uses such a phrase to express the word *heaven* in the new language, it is quite likely that the people will attach those associations with the word *heaven* and believe that Christian teaching sets that out as a fact and says "God dwells above the clouds." On the other hand, if a particular culture thought that God dwells in a stream or a river and had a word for this place, then a translator would be faced with using this word for heaven. There would be a danger of portraying God as dwelling within nature. Such dilemmas always face the translator of Scripture and liturgy from one language to another.

A universal liturgy

The alternative, which can seem more attractive to the originating Church, is to retain the words of their own liturgy and use this as a universal liturgy. Each new group of Christians would need to learn the language of this liturgy, and in time it would become "the tradition." This approach offers a sense of continuity with history, although many worshipers would not be aware of the beginning point of this history. The other main advantage for this approach is that people of many different languages and cultures can come together on equal terms and worship as one group of Christians in what is considered "the Christian language."

However, I doubt that all the worshipers have the same concepts in their minds even when they use the same words. Each culture will color the words with its own interpretations, based on the assumed understandings of the key concepts. This probably applies to us all as individuals to some extent, although if there is good teaching about the meaning of the liturgy and the doctrines of the Church, we can share much in common.

A liturgy appropriate for each culture, age, and gender

Having considered briefly the problems of translating Christian concepts from one language to another for their use in the liturgy of the local Church, we can look at the reasons why it is important that a liturgy reflect the culture, gender, and age of the worshipers.

My experience in attending many different worship occasions while writing this book was that the people at worship considered Christ to be "one of us" and identified strongly with the Christ who they believed understood their particular needs and situations. If the liturgy is expressed in an unfamiliar type of language and form, then such identification is harder to achieve. Christ is not seen as belonging to us, and God becomes remote and distant. The strong emphasis on the doctrine of the Incarnation in modern times has borne fruit in acknowledging that God is very concerned for our world and for each individual within it. This has led to increasing pressure to reflect such identification of God with us in the way the liturgy of worship is expressed for each particular culture, age, and gender.

In attempts to write liturgies for children or youth, the authors use language and concepts particularly relevant to people in those age groups. The aim is to assist that particular group of people to create a bond with Christ within their own age and culture. The liturgy creates the concept that God so understands the language of the group that God surely identifies with them and their life situation. If a different language and style are used, then the implication is that God is not "one of us" and is not interested in the affairs of the group.

But there are two disadvantages in writing such liturgies. The first is that it implies that worship is only for a small group of people, whereas worship within the Christian Church is always representative of the whole people of God. A group of Christians never worships alone but always in the company of the saints, both on earth and in heaven. Many churches have insisted on a universally recognized ministry in order to emphasize that worship is both universal and local. The priest makes sure that the whole Church is acknowledged as well as the local congregation in the celebration of the Eucharist and in the administration of the sacrament of baptism. Whenever a liturgy becomes too particular in style and language, it begins to be exclusive rather than inclusive.

The second disadvantage is that if the principle of a different liturgy for each different group is followed to its logical conclusion, an endless number of liturgies would be needed as the group of worshipers changed on each occasion. In the end, as I have indicated previously, each individual would need to have a liturgy in his or her own style and language, and that would be suitable only for their individual worship. Following our previous line of thinking, Christ would become so much "like me" that he could not relate to any other person on equal terms.

A liturgy for all

An attempt must be made to balance the need for universal worship, using a widely accepted form of language, with the need for worship suited to a particular culture, age, and gender, using language and form with which the worshiper can easily relate. It is possible that the early Church has useful examples for our generation. In the first centuries, freedom was given to the presider of the assembly to express certain local petitions and thanksgiving within a structure that required the other parts of the liturgy to be in the universal language. This method tried to safeguard the doctrine of the Church while at the same time allowing the expression of local needs. It declared to the worshiper that the liturgy belonged to the universal Church but that God was also identified with local concerns.

In the end the twofold rule for the use of liturgy within the Church must be that it sets out the true nature of God and the work of Christ, and that it does not exclude any worshiper by the language it uses. The use of inclusive language in terms of gender is vital to satisfy the latter of these two principles. It is not acceptable to use language that refers to the human race as if it is all male. The use of the word *men* is no longer suitable as an equivalent for human beings of all ages and both genders. The word *men* excludes both women, girls, and boys. The liturgy must be so written as to make certain that all the worshipers in the congregation feel that they are included.

NB

I believe that the acceptance of the doctrine of the Ascension helped the early Church to free itself from the patterns of a fixed place, a fixed language, and a fixed style for worship. It allowed each group of Christians to lift their hearts to heaven and worship with and through Christ. Each group of Christians could bring their own culture and experience into their worship and add these to the richness of the whole. They could imagine Christ in their situation, through the power of the Spirit, and look for his guidance and response. Such a Christ would always be the Christ who had become part of their world through his Incarnation in a particular place, time, and human form. It would be the Christ who brought them salvation through the historical events of the Cross and Resurrection. It would be the Christ who ascended beyond time and space to pioneer for them the new life of eternity. Yet it was the Christ who now met them in their own place and culture. The Christ of history had become for them the Christ of worship, their own contemporary and the contemporary of every culture and race.

Multicultural worship

As people of many different cultures move globally from one place to another with increasing frequency, our worship should also reflect the multicultural nature of the Christian Church. The language, art, cultural symbols, and customs of all who gather regularly for worship should find expression in the liturgy of the Church in any particular location. It was a delight to see this mixture of peoples in many places I visited during the pilgrimage. Such a mixture expresses the concept of the worldwide Church for many local congregations. However, worship leaders will have to work harder in many places to add touches of the "wider" cultures to the predominant culture of the local Church.

I can see many possibilities to achieve this principle.

- For example, the Scriptures can be read in a variety of languages as long as adequate written translations are available for those who do not know the language of the reader. Overhead projection of such translations is an increasing practice.

- In the intercessions, a person from one culture can often fill in the background of a petition for those of other cultures who are present and who do not understand the issues involved. A variety of languages can also be used in the intercessions, especially if there is a printed order for the people to follow.
- In the distribution of Communion, lay assistants could be chosen from a variety of cultures and, if appropriate, wear their distinctive cultural dress. The Church Universal will then be more visible in each locality, and all present will be full participants.
- In the music and songs, the diversity can again become audible through the variety of languages used. The congregation at Soweto proved to me that it is possible to be united in the musical tune while at the same time being particular in the words of the different language groups. The same was demonstrated at the ecumenical center at Taizé.

We live in a multicultural society, so our worship needs to honor the varieties of culture. Our places of worship also need to be adorned with liturgical art that reflects such variety. At the Lambeth Conference of Anglican Bishops in 1988, stunning use was made of liturgical art projected onto plain painted walls in the worship space as an aid to our reverence and devotion. This use of modern technology should be harnessed as much for visual art as for sound where the use of the microphone and recording equipment is widespread even in small churches. Through such technology we can adjust the visual art to the size of our worship space and can vary it from season to season in accordance with the theme of the service.

The dilemma for the artists

The writers of liturgy had to hold deeply to the truth in the Ascension doctrine. So also did the creators of liturgical art. There the issue gains a sharper focus. Can artists be true to the historical situation when they have few details of the original features of the people or the scene? No one seems to have thought that a record should be kept of the facial likeness of Jesus Christ. The same is true about the apostles or the family of Jesus. Because of this, artists have a wonderful freedom to show in the expression of the features what they believe best portrays the qualities of the person. The features, therefore, become symbolic of the true inner nature of that person.

Christian artists have also developed the use of key symbols to show the connection between the person and the historical events. The relationship of Madonna and Child represented the Incarnation, and the relationship between Christ and the cross represented the Crucifixion. The Resurrection has been more variously shown, sometimes with the open tomb as the symbol and sometimes with a background of light. The Ascension has been even more difficult to symbolize, although many artists have used the cloud or the upward gaze of the disciples as their sign of this event.

The importance of the use of symbol

The scene is understood by worshipers because of the symbol, not because they recognize a standard portrait of the figure of Christ. It is the symbol that shows that it is Christ and what activity is occurring. We have become so used to this idea that it is often hard for us to see its importance. It has given artists wonderful freedom to express Christ as a fellow human being without the limitations of actuality.

Artists have used such freedom to incorporate contemporary clothing and backgrounds into the biblical scenes. This makes us feel that Jesus is living, speaking, and working in our contemporary situation. It reinforces the principle of Christ being "one of us." The artist retains the symbol associated with the event as the connection with the historical occurrence and then feels free to use contemporary people and places in the scene. Some artists have clearly chosen to portray their own local area as the background for a biblical scene. Local geography and sometimes even domestic furniture are used. They do not see the need to try to recapture the buildings of Jerusalem or the geography of Israel. They also do not try to find out what sort of clothing might have been worn by the people in the scene or the style of the furnishings.

The face of Christ

On this principle it was possible for artists to portray key figures with the faces and features of people known to them. If the disciples were people just like us, then artists could use their friends or enemies as models of the key characters. They could even paint or carve the face of Christ from their imagination of how a person of his nature would look or from the example of the person who was most Christlike. They were therefore able to see Christ as belonging to their racial or cultural group.

There seemed to be little difficulty in this approach while the features of the artist's race were roughly similar to those of the characters in the Scriptures. The Mediterranean peoples and the peoples of Europe were not too dissimilar in features. Once the Christian faith took hold in China, India, Africa, South America, and the Pacific, the color and the eye configuration were distinctive. The question as to whether a contemporary figure of Christ would be true to the Christ of history then became important. Could an African Christ be a true symbol of the Savior of all peoples? Can the particular represent the universal when the universal is so diverse?

The picture and the photograph

The question has been complicated by the processes of printing and photography. The process of printing pictures meant that missionaries of the nineteenth century were able to take cheap copies of paintings of biblical scenes with them as they spread the gospel on other continents. Those who listened to the stories had no idea whether this was a picture of the person of Christ or just the artist's perception of the person of Christ. The listeners would probably have thought that if the artist had drawn a beard, then Christ must have had a beard; if the artist had depicted certain clothes, then Christ must have worn those clothes; if the artist showed Christ with a pale white face, then Christ must have come from such a race.

This confusion was compounded by the use of photography. Here was the production of "true images." What was the difference between a photograph and a printed painting? Was one a true likeness and the other an artist's impression? How could one tell the difference? Numerous people on many continents began to forget the principles that had governed liturgical art and started to make comparisons with the true image of photograph. A printed picture of Jesus meant that he must have looked like that, that he wore those clothes, and that his skin was that color. The Jesus of worship must be compared with the Jesus of supposed history. This isolated the Christ of worship from the contemporary situation of the worshiper. The Christ was not "one of us" but one of them— either of a different race or time or culture.

The cultural Christ

Attempts have been made, particularly in India, China, and Africa, to show Christ as belonging to the culture of the artist. I have seen a wonderful example of this in the chapel of the bishop's house in Johannesburg. The carving, which came from the Masai tribal area of Tanzania, was of a man of mature age from one particular tribe. The teeth are filed in a certain way and the loincloth has the exact cultural pattern on it. Yet the man clearly represents Jesus, for the figure is nailed to a cross.

Thus we have the combination of the cultural and the historical in this masterpiece of liturgical carving. It is of universal appeal as well as of local significance. The Christ who brings salvation to every nation is identified with a particular nation and tribe. It is true that the particularity could limit the attraction of this symbol to those of that tribe, and there is always the danger of making Christ so tribal that others cannot relate to the Christ as "one of us." For this reason there are those who would never define the face or feature of the Christ on the cross. They want them to remain a mystery so that worshipers can fill in the details from their own imagination. This approach has its merits, but the theology of the Incarnation makes us long for a positive identification with the human race rather than assigning worship solely to the realm of mystery.

The gender of Christ on the cross

As I met people during the course of this study, I asked for a response to the possibility of an artist portraying Christ as a female figure on the cross. I prefaced this suggestion with reference to the various examples of cultural figures of a male Christ that I had seen. Most replies applauded the attempts by artists to represent Christ as belonging to their particular culture but shrank from any positive response to Christ being shown in female form. The respondents were both male and female, holding a variety of progressive and conservative attitudes. Some, of course, reacted emotionally to such a radical idea, but others gave it more thought and were able to articulate the reasons for their response.

These replies mostly referred to the Incarnation principle that Jesus Christ was male but claimed as such to be a true representative of the whole of humanity. Similarly, no one I met wanted to confuse the gender of Mary, the Mother of the Lord. In their understanding, the maleness of Jesus did not prevent our identification with the Christ as one with *all* humanity. Some respondents saw advantage in portraying Christ in a form particular to the culture of his own people in Israel; then the historical connections of gender and race in the Incarnation would be maintained. The Christ, particularly if we follow the doctrine of the Ascension, would then represent the whole of humanity through the particularity of the one person Jesus Christ. The particular would encompass the universal.

For others there is a real advantage in having a variety of artistic representations of Christ. Then all peoples can be assured that they can relate to the ascended Lord, who understands their human situation within their own context. However, this same principle did not appeal to many when it came to be applied to the gender of the Christ on the cross.

Another avenue open to the artist would be to not make the figure of Christ on the cross gender specific, but at that point the identity with real humanity begins to be lost. I believe that the widespread use of the naked figure of the male child in the Incarnation scene is a sign of the theological importance of portraying Jesus as born a full human being and male in gender. It signifies that Jesus is a real human being like us and not a neutral demi-God. In the same way, the suffering human figure shown on the cross is clearly male, and the pain, the shame, and the agony are there for all to see. The artist is affirming the truth, which the theologians have expressed in the Creeds, that Jesus in the Incarnation became fully human and shared the common trials of our existence.

The damage at the Reformation

The zeal of the iconoclasts at the Reformation to remove any representation of the divine in human form not only robbed future generations of some wonderful examples of liturgical art but also allowed worshipers to forget that Jesus was indeed like them in all respects except without sin (see Heb 4:15). It is possible that this added to the common picture, held by many in the last hundred years, of the Christ as a God walking the earth without hardly touching the ground and far too holy to see the awful things that afflict the human condition. The stained-glass windows of the period have an anemic Christ who seems to float just above the earth, dressed in flowing garments that no contemporary would be wearing, looking totally remote and innocent of all reality. The scene may show a sign of blessing by Christ, but that action is unrelated to any human need.

The cross without a Christ

The Evangelical section of the Church has often emphasized that the plain cross, without any human figure on it, was the presentation of the empty cross of the Resurrection. When this statement is considered from a critical point of view, it becomes obvious that there is a serious confusion of symbol. The cross is the defined symbol of crucifixion and salvation. It is identified with the victory of love over hatred, of forgiveness over sin, and of the sacrifice of obedience and accepted suffering. It cannot also be the symbol of the Resurrection. That symbol is the standing Christ revealing the scars of the cross. The appearance of light conquering darkness may be added, and on occasion the tomb with the stone rolled away. However, the time of the cross is past, and it should not appear again in a true Easter representation.

The influence of art on worship

All this prevailing liturgical art has a very profound effect on the attitudes of the worshiper. If the symbols do not recall the Christ of history, then the mystical Christ of worship will be so powerful that the reality and humanity of Christ will be quickly lost. The wonder of the Ascension doctrine is that it holds together the truth that the fullness of the humanity of Christ is within the divine Lord. The worshiper can envision the Christ in heaven as fully human and fully divine, who with the power and responsibility of God can share our basic experiences as human beings.

It is for this reason that I do not advocate religious art departing from the norm of showing the figure on the cross as male. To do so would be to let go of the historical truth to such an extent that we could create any type of "myth" to aid our worship. The Christian religion, unlike most others, centers itself on the revelation of God in history. To portray Christ as female is to deny the reality of the Incarnation. However, the point that we have learned from this study of the Ascension doctrine is that this young, male, Jewish Jesus is the representative for us of all humanity in all the essentials of being human. When the artist shows the figure as male, the worshiper, whether male or female, should feel close to the humanness rather than to the gender of this person. I believe we have already done this as regards age and race, and we can equally reconcile the issue of gender.

Ideally, like a young boy I met on my pilgrimage to Soweto, we should be able to identify the Christ whatever the shade of skin color. The most helpful artistry in such a situation is probably to show a variety of shades and move away from the monochrome, pale white of the Anglo-Saxon Christ. I find the tribal representation of Christ just as hard to support as a female Christ, however much I am attracted to the beauty of the work. My experience on my pilgrimage was that the worshipers made their own association with Christ as "one of us" by transferring the model of the artist to their own situation. The most successful model of Christ by an artist will be the one that best stimulates this involvement by the worshiper. Christians are now rightly sensitive to the issues of race, culture, and gender, so artists will need to be more thoughtful in the way that the Incarnation connection is retained.

A sensitive and sensible debate

I admit that this is a most difficult issue to pursue with logic. I believe it should be the subject of much wider debate between theologians and artists, and between both these groups and the general worshiping congregation. My hope is that this book might be a stimulus to this debate. The purpose of the debate must always be focused on the question: How can the artist best assist the worshipers to lift their hearts to heaven to worship the ascended Christ in spirit and in truth? As we continue with this debate, we must find words to express our feelings as well as our logic and our theology, for our emotions have a proper place in any future liturgical debate.

Practical implications for the future

The visual arts

As we look to the future of worship in the new millennium, we will expect to be able to rejoice in the treasures of the past as well as provide contemporary channels for our worship.

To make the best use of the liturgical art of the past, we need to be provided with knowledge of the context and the principles that lie behind the artist's work, whether that be in mosaic, painting, sculpture, stained glass, or ceramics. Hearing the explanations by the Franciscan Brothers who acted as our guides in the basilica in Assisi, we gained greater appreciation of the frescoes painted by Giotto. We began to understand the new theological insights of God that these paintings gave. We could see that belief in a God who is personal and close to the ordinary Christian permeated the paintings. These showed the domestic architecture and hills familiar to the pilgrim at a ceiling height to which they could relate. We also understood the point of the additional figures and animals in the Last Supper scene. Without this sort of explanation from a guide, we would have taken offense at the intrusion of non-historical material in the portraits of Christ and the disciples. The same point can be made about the painting in the Resurrection Chapel in the National Cathedral in Washington, where the artist has included contemporary portraits as disciples. Even the glass-mirrored Christ icon in a church in Toronto was acceptable to a degree, once the positive point of the theology was made clear—that the faithful are also part of the visible body of Christ.

The guide, then, whether oral or written, becomes an important aid in making liturgical art a springboard for effective worship. Too often the art is allowed to die without a living voice of commentary, and in such a state it only adds to the depression of the worshiper.

My plea, as far as new liturgical art is concerned, is for boldness and a clarity of image that is evocative to the heart and mind of the viewer. It needs to be informed by a deep measure of theological understanding and speak more of God than the passing social context. Too much "memorial" art highlights the human person(s) to be remembered, and this weakens the priority of the divine dimension. In my opinion, the place for the memorial is on a separate tablet rather than on the artwork itself.

My further plea to those responsible for designing liturgical space in the future is that they allow a significant measure of natural light and view into the worship area. Too many of the great buildings that have been erected for worship have become gloomy and dark. Every window, wall, and space has been filled with liturgical art of one generation or another. Medical research has pointed out the valuable properties of sunshine and light in helping to lift the spirits of people. I find it significant that Jesus used the open-air setting for some of his teaching, especially for larger crowds in Galilee. Some of his own times of prayer and reflection were in places open to the sun and the sky. In making the point, I am not advocating open-air settings as better for regular worship. I am well aware of the wisdom of Christians down the generations in showing the value of a building to house our continuing memory of God's presence in the variety of occasions for worship, whatever the weather might be. What I am advocating is that our worship space should be a place of light, warmth, color, and peacefulness. Our liturgical art must contribute and enhance this objective.

In the future, liturgical art can make significant use of modern technology not only for the purposes of lighting but also to provide images that can be adapted to suit the occasion. The poster and the banner have been frequently used in recent years as seasonal adornments in our churches. They have a place in artistic work but often lack the clarity and vitality of stained glass or full painting. Given that these latter are expensive and therefore more permanent, there must be room for a more flexible and less expensive form of art. This can be provided by projection onto a suitable wall or screen. Such projection must not dominate other essential liturgical symbols, but it can be very evocative if used correctly.

A major symbol in the Church has regained its proper theological prominence in recent years. It is the font or bath for baptism. The real symbolism of baptism lies in the water rather than its receptacle, but this is only obvious during the time of the baptism itself. However, it would enhance this vital sacrament if liturgical art were able to heighten our awareness of the symbol of water as the spring of new life in Christ. Too often art has portrayed the opposite of new life by adding heavy ornamentation to the stonework of the font or, even worse, to an elaborate lid fitted to close the top of the font. If the symbol of water could be made visible for many to see when the font is not in actual use, then the theological truth of baptism would be more obvious as a permanent feature of the worship space.

In addition to water, wine and bread are common objects in many cultures, and that is no doubt why Christ chose them as the substance of the sacraments that the ascended Lord left us as earthly foretastes of the heavenly life. These substances have provided wonderful opportunities for artists to give visible expression to the sacraments in the variety of cultures where the Christian faith has taken root. As new cultures are incorporated into many local churches, showing that the global village is now a reality in many places, art forms to represent these cultures will also need a place in those churches. The example of the Church of the Annunciation at Nazareth shows that the key to this will lie in being inclusive and in allowing variety within the one space. On the grounds of due economy, I think that the use of projection technology will be helpful in providing a means of gathering a variety of cultural representations without heavy cost.

Many Christians associate peace and beauty with the picture of heaven. I believe that they are good tests of the appropriateness of liturgical art in our places of worship. For the Roman Catholic community, the reforms of Vatican II provided an opportunity to take a critical look at the adornment and shape appropriate for their liturgical space. The freedom that those reforms gave to local parishes to sort out their priorities and needs is still evident in many of the churches I saw on my visit to the continent of Europe. A sense of beauty and movement has been created in some of these churches by the use of simple long strips of material from near the ceiling to the floor to highlight a liturgical symbol. Focused lighting has been added. If plain sheeting is used, the illumination could be with colored lighting, varied from season to season. Even the hung material is a symbol of the joining of heaven and earth in a single fold. In such places I found these symbols a clear inspiration for my worship, and look forward to seeing them more widely used in the new millennium.

Floral art

The use of floral art has done much to add beauty to our worship spaces over many generations. New skills in floral art have been created in recent times. Many of these use the advances of modern technology. The height of the arrangement is no longer restricted by the height of the container. Columns of flowers can be arranged to match the size of the worship space. Foliage and flowers can be combined with stunning effect. There has been very sensitive use of the floral arrangement to enhance the sacramental symbolism rather than detract from it. It would be good if in the future we will not see flowers smothering the font or the altar.

The choice of materials for the floral decorations can add a seasonal touch to the worship space as a whole. Spring flowers in the Northern Hemisphere can reflect the new life of Easter, and the colors of the displays can match those for the feast. The scent of the flowers can add another bodily dimension to the worship, particularly in those churches that do not use incense.

Flowers can have their own symbolism as established in liturgical art. Again, explanations may be needed, but once the symbolism is understood, it is another aid to worship. The crocus, the lily, the myrtle, and the rose can all carry their own meaning.

The use of flowers should continue to help the worshiper connect the Creator with God's children and remind us of our responsibility for the conservation of the tender things in God's world.

Music

The psalms tell us that music has enhanced worship since earliest times. The musical setting can mirror all the emotions associated with the different parts of worship: praise, adoration, penitence, pardon, thanksgiving, pleas for courage, understanding, empowerment, and peace. Music can both remind us of past associations and also lead us on into new experiences of the divine. It stirs the heart and fires the conscience.

In most churches the principal musical instrument, be it an organ or a piano, is the most costly piece of equipment in the worship space. It is a delight to see the musical revival that is training young people to play such instruments. It is important, though, for the music to be supported rather than dominated by the principal instrument and for other musical talents among the congregation to be included. The flute, violin, and trumpet have been found to add a distinctive tone to worship in accordance with the need. The solo voice or the unaccompanied choir must not be overlooked. It has been a surprise to many that recordings of plainsong have become so popular in the developed world. All this points to the need to incorporate as much variety as possible into our worship so that there may be full participation with excellence of skill.

Music is closely connected with culture and can often express culture most effectively. In my own country of New Zealand, the Maori people, who are naturally musical, have given voice to much of their Christian faith through the unaccompanied singing of hymns in their own language and cultural style.

The Charismatic Renewal has developed extensive use of music as an aid to the experience of the Holy Spirit during worship. It is used to stir the energy at one time and still the heart at other times so that there may be awareness of the movement of the Holy Spirit.

The future use of such music will depend on the composition of words that satisfy the mind. It is vital that we maintain good theology in the words of our songs and hymns, because the mem-

NB 1

ory retains what we sing to music much longer than the words we use in speech.

One of the key factors in worship is the balance that can be achieved between the various high points in any service and in the energy level that can be sustained by the congregation. The worship leaders of the future will assist us in effective worship if they can regulate the musical input to provide a balance for our various moods. We need both to be energized for participation and to be relaxed for those moments when we want to regain our strength for the next highlight in the worship service.

With modern sound technology, there is increasing use of background music in preparation for worship and to support an activity during worship. This use could be extended to those times when there is not a worship service in the church. There are now so many visitors and pilgrims who come to our churches as places of public interest and beauty that a building needs to be brought to life both by music and symbol. A partially lit church with quiet music playing has a vitality about it that turns it from a museum into a place hallowed by the worship of generations. So pilgrims are encouraged to add their own prayers and find new strength for their journey to heaven.

Summary

In this chapter I have set out what I see as some of the pressing issues raised by this study of the doctrine of the Ascension as it affects the use of liturgy and liturgical art in our times. I have sought to hold the balance between the need for a universal liturgy in which people of all cultures and ages and both genders can equally share and the proper recognition that the language of the liturgy must be that of the people involved so that they can fully identify with the Christ of worship. I have added my practical suggestions for enlivening our worship with the treasures of other cultures, with art, and with music. I have surveyed the dilemmas that face the liturgical artist of our day and highlighted the difficulties of portraying Christ. I have recognized the need to portray personal features and how hard it is to do this without being tied to those of the race and gender of Christ's Incarnation.

I have emphasized how the doctrine of the Ascension can assist the worshiper to move beyond the time and space of the Incarnation and relate to the Christ as the one who represents every person who is human and the one who shares in that humanity in all the essentials of the human condition. Thus the worshiper should be able to hold the Christ of worship in full relationship to the Christ of history.

I encourage a full debate between theologians, artists, and worshipers on these key issues and trust that such a debate will be conducted with sense and sensibility.

CHAPTER 9

Conclusion: Personal Implications of the Doctrine of the Ascension

The review of the contents of this book shows me how the doctrine of the Ascension applies to so many areas of Christian thought, worship, and action. We have seen that it has implications for our understanding of what it means to be human. It has developed thinking about the "character" of God. It has influenced the way we say our prayers and shape the liturgy. It has caused a review of the future of worship as the new millennium begins. It has challenged us to rethink the future of our existence after death. It has showed us new insights into many passages of Scripture that are often regarded as difficult to interpret. Finally, it has even drawn our attention to the fact that in a scientific age we have to learn again the art of seeing the truth in symbolism.

The window at Taizé

As I draw my writing to a close, my mind goes back to my response to that time of reflection in front of the Ascension window at Taizé that I described in Chapter 2 (p. 25). There I found myself asking this deep question:

How will I take my part in carrying the world, transforming it and loving it? As I pondered an answer, my thinking focused on action. Thus it was inevitable that in this Conclusion I should explore the personal implications of the Ascension doctrine.

Christ in action

Once you have studied the Ascension and the doctrine that developed from it, the only way to think of the ascended Christ is to see Christ in action. Too often we have spoken of the historical Christ and the heavenly Christ as if Christ is the "object" in the sentence. Christ seems to have become the object of our study, our thinking, and, in prayer, our requests. We must refocus our minds to see Christ as the subject—the Christ of action. Then we shall be able to say that:

> Christ prays,
> Christ cares,
> Christ works for the fulfillment of the purposes of God,
> Christ is the initiator.

Like a master craftsman, Christ shapes the future of the world. Through the Ascension we realize that Christ has accepted full responsibility for the outcomes of God's plan for the universe.

As the new millennium begins and the future century stretches before us, it is easy to focus on human achievement and human planning. With the Ascension doctrine in mind, Christians can reaffirm that the future, first of all, is in God's hands. God has a design for what should be achieved. There is a divine agenda. What the New Testament calls the Kingdom of God is being brought to fulfillment through the prayer and activity of Christ. To state it firmly again, the ascended Christ is active in all this, not passive!

Humanity in action

This renewed vision of the work of the ascended Christ challenges us all to respond with our human activity. What shall we do to be partners of Christ?

Partners in prayer

First, we will be partners in active prayer. We will lend our spiritual strength and support to the intercessions of Christ. Such prayer will not only release spiritual energy into the world but will empower our own activity. The media at the millennium have exposed us to the heat of the great problems that face humanity in every part of the globe. We hear of every disaster, every prophet of doom, every possibility of destruction, every crime of humanity, and every twist of fate. With the intensity of such media heat, we wither and faint. Our corporate actions in response seem so feeble. The good are so quickly overpowered by evil. The ranks of the faithful seem to be so thin. Only as we reaffirm the vision of the Christ at work and at prayer for us will we be able to take courage and plan for the future. This is part of the outcome of our prayers.

Partners in planning

Secondly, we will be partners in planning. The Cross, the Resurrection, and the Ascension all demonstrate the planning of God and the preparedness of Jesus. Things are not left to chance in the divine/human story. We too, as human beings, must include planning as part of the activity of discipleship. We will examine the issues carefully and then plan our response with diligence. At the beginning of every new period of time, be it a year, a century, or a millennium, there is a human desire to look forward and to plan. Christians should stimulate such work and share fully in it.

In our planning we look for the guidance of the Scriptures and models among our forebears in the Christian faith. Our examination of the Scriptures will identify the principles on which we will act. It will remind us of the overall objective of God's creation: *shalom.* It is difficult to translate this Hebrew word, for it incorporates many ideas. Shalom brings together the concepts of harmony, peace, truth, justice, and hope within the framework of wholeness. When there is shalom, all things fit into their proper place in relation to God and all other things. Also included in the concept of shalom is respect. There is shalom when human beings respect one another and all other creatures and matter in God's creation. When there is shalom, God is at the center of all things, all plans, and all activity.

Partners in action

Thirdly, we are partners in action with Christ. The Ascension helps us to see that with the power of Christ enabling us, we can take up our responsibility to be full participants in the activity of building the Kingdom. Our activity will not be frozen into inertia because the tasks seem so great. As in our prayers of intercession, we will learn to do our part and trust Christ to oversee the whole.

We have also learned from this study of the Ascension that our actions must be based on the principle of redemptive love—and on no other. To use again the words of the writer of the Book of Revelation: "Then I saw between the throne and the four living creatures and among the elders a Lamb standing as if it had been slaughtered" (Rev 5:6). When as humans we think of action, too often we become militant. We are enthused by power and become overpowering. The principle of redemptive love forbids us to overpower anyone or anything. Instead, our activity is aimed at empowering others so that they can find a redeemed life through love. We love them enough to want the best for them for their own sake. All our activity is geared to help them find new and fulfilling ways of living well.

Partners in thanksgiving

Finally, we are partners in thanksgiving. When we have put our plans into action and see the fruits of our work and noted our achievements, then our response will be a shout of praise and a tumble of thanksgiving. As corporate humanity, we will give thanks to God. With joy we will take our place in the presence of God and express our words of thanks. In such an attitude pride can never have pride of place. Thanksgiving will keep us humble. This does not mean that we will denigrate the part we have played in the achievements we note. Humility, like shalom, recognizes the proper part each has played.

We will acknowledge the initiatives of the ascended Christ. We will know that we have been empowered by Christ's prayer. We will mark the inspiration of the Word of God in Scripture. We will rejoice in the gifts of the ascended Christ given to us for the good of all. We will humbly share with God the role that we have played in reaching these outcomes. And God will rejoice with us. God will offer thanks to us. God will want to see us receive our proper share of the praise and the reward. That reward will be to know that good things have been achieved for the welfare of the whole human race. Thus our activity and our thanksgiving will create shalom, each part fitting fully to create a perfect whole.

Individuals in action

As individuals we will share fully in these corporate actions. We will also find that there are practical outcomes of the Ascension doctrine for each one of us personally. Of the many, there are two that I would like to share with you in this final section of the Conclusion.

1. Respect for Jesus Christ

This study has helped me have a new "respect" for Jesus Christ. It has warmed my faith, given me a new vision, and helped me develop a deeper relationship with this Christ. It has been important to reaffirm that the ascended Christ still retains the human experience. I feel that I can share my humanity more fully with Christ in prayer. The reflection on the theological implications has helped me gain a fuller respect for the divinity of Christ, united in the one personhood. I have been able to relate to such a person without creating either a superman or a super-God. My respect for Christ has given me new respect for myself and new energy for prayer and worship. This study has made me more aware of the actions of Christ and the fulfillment of the purposes of God. I have a greater confidence and a fuller hope.

2. Respect for my fellow human beings

The words of Archbishop Desmond Tutu that I quoted on page 79 made me realize that the Ascension doctrine has very practical implications for my relationships with other human beings. The diversity of culture, gender, age, and race is dominant in my own community. As more emphasis is put on our differences, I began to wonder what we had in common as human beings. It is easy to shrink within oneself and build up a defensive wall toward this diversity. If we have nothing in common, then I need feel little responsibility for my diverse neighbors.

This study of the Ascension and the insights of Archbishop Tutu have given me cause to take a new look at my neighbors and new strength to respect them. By respect I mean that I see my neighbor as:

- a child of the same creator God;
- a partner in working for the good of all;
- the source and the need of mutual interdependent care;
- a fellow human being with many of the same feelings, fears, and hopes I have;
- different from me and therefore having a distinctive contribution to make to the whole community;
- one, like me, in struggling to make sense of self and God.

Such respect allows me to share our commonality and note our differences with equal emphasis. Like my respect for the ascended Christ, fully human and fully divine, my respect for my neighbor will hold together what is common to our humanity and what is distinctive in our gender, age, culture, and race. I cannot be one without the other, and the two are held together within the one person. The one does not deny the other but incarnates it in the uniqueness of the person who I am.

What answer can I give?

Such personal and practical implications are a sure sign of the value of theological thinking. They help us unite earth and heaven, prayer and action, love of God and love of self and neighbor. So when someone says to me, "What does the Ascension mean for you?" I have a lot to say! May some of what I have written be useful as you personally discover your own response to the prayers and work of the ascended Christ, our Savior and our Lord.

CHAPTER 10

Appendix: The Geography of the Ascension

LUKE'S ASCENSION LOCATION— SHORT NOTE ON LUKE 24:50[1]

While undertaking research for this book on the Ascension and its implications for worship in the multicultural setting of today's Church, I studied in detail the location of the Ascension as described by the author of Luke 24:50-53 and Acts 1:6-12. The recorded sites vary in the two accounts, which is surprising, since most scholars agree that the same author is responsible for both books.[2]

In Luke 24:50 the location is attached to the village of Bethany: "Then he led them out as far as Bethany, and, lifting up his hands, he blessed them."

In Acts 1:12 the disciples, after the Ascension scene, return from the Mount of Olives: "Then they returned to Jerusalem from the mount called Olivet, which is near Jerusalem, a sabbath day's journey away."

Is Luke here referring to the same location but using two different descriptions to make narrative links with other material in

1. This note was first published in *The Expository Times* (April 1998), vol. 109, no. 7.

2. For example, see *New Views on Luke and Acts*, ed. Earl Richard (Collegeville, Minn.: The Liturgical Press, 1990) 15–32; Robert C. Tannehill, *The Narrative Unity of Luke-Acts: A Literary Interpretation*, 2 vols., Foundations and Facets (Minneapolis: Fortress Press, 1990) 2:6–8. For a fuller argument on the issues of unity see Mikeal C. Parsons and Richard I. Pervo, *Rethinking the Unity of Luke and Acts* (Minneapolis: Fortress Press, 1993).

the Gospel and Acts respectively, or is he indicating that he had found two different locations among the traditions in the early Church?[3] My preference is for the first alternative.

In the Gospel the road to Bethany is associated with the entry into Jerusalem as described in Luke 19:29: "When he had come near Bethphage and Bethany, at the place called the Mount of Olives, he sent two of his disciples. . . ." By showing that the departure and blessing of the disciples were at the same place as the entry into Jerusalem, Luke crowns the triumphal entry with the triumphal exit of Christ. The Gospel narrative is crisply brought to completion by the cycle of association with the same geographical place. The purpose of the entry into Jerusalem by the Son of Man was to bring to birth the Kingdom of God. At the Ascension God's purpose was fulfilled. Then the disciples took on the responsibility, with Christ's blessing, of being the messengers of the salvation wrought by Christ on the cross and affirmed through his resurrection. Luke's first volume ends with this hope, and in the second volume this hope becomes reality in the acts of the apostles.

In Acts the author indicates that the Ascension took place "on the mount called Olivet," linking the Ascension with the experience of Jesus in the garden at its foot. There Jesus prayed for God's will to be done; and there the disciples had fallen asleep and deserted Jesus when he needed them to share the crisis (Luke 22:39-46). Through the common reference to the Mount of Olives, the author makes the contrast clear. The disciples' final memory of Jesus is positive. He empowers them for obedient service. Like Jesus, the disciples discover the power of prayer to fulfill God's purpose. That is the record of the Acts of the Apostles.

So we can see why the author, for narrative reasons, wants to retain two different place names for the one Ascension event.

My research in Jerusalem caused me to examine the geographical locations on the ground. From an early date tradition has the site of the Ascension on a ridge running along the top of the Mount of

---

3. For a full discussion on all the variations in the Ascension narratives in the Gospel and in Acts, see Mikeal C. Parsons, *The Departure of Jesus in Luke-Acts,* Journal for the Study of the New Testament, Supplement Series 21 (Sheffield: JSOT Press, 1987).

Olives. At the foot of the ridge is the olive garden at Gethsemane. A narrow road still leads down the ridge from Bethphage to this garden. On the reverse slope the road winds down to Bethany. Is this the ridge that Luke refers to by two different signposts? C. K. Barrett quotes Dalman as believing that "the traditional location somewhat north of the Bethany road, on the full height of the summit looking towards Jerusalem, would suit all the data."[4]

Marshall sees no obvious reason for a conscious change of location in Acts. He believes that Luke closely associated Bethany and the Mount of Olives (cf. Luke 19:29) and explains the use of Bethany in Luke 24:50 as Luke using the one name known to him.[5] However, Dunn points to the eschatological significance of the Mount of Olives in Acts to highlight the restoration of the Kingdom and the final return in Acts 1:6-11.[6] Part of the slopes of the Mount of Olives is even now covered with graves ready to greet the Messiah at the end of the age.

Can we, then, read the prepositions in the Greek text of Luke 24:50 to make sense of this suggested location for the Ascension? The variants read:

> 50 . . . αὐτοὺς ἕως πρὸς Βηθανίαν
> or . . . αὐτοὺς ἕως εἰς Βηθανίαν
> or . . . αὐτοὺς ἔξω ἕως πρὸς Βηθανίαν [7]

The difficult word is ἕως. The dictionaries translate this as "up to this point" and sometimes as "till within." With πρός or εἰς it usually means "as far as." So three Bible translations give "out as far as Bethany." In the light of our discussion of Luke 19:29, does this mean that Luke considered that the district of Bethany began

4. C. K. Barrett, *A Critical and Exegetical Commentary on the Acts of the Apostles,* International Critical Commentary on the Holy Scriptures of the Old and New Testament 34 (Edinburgh: T & T Clark, 1994) 85.

5. I. Howard Marshall, *The Acts of the Apostles: An Introduction and Commentary,* The Tyndale New Testament Commentaries (Grand Rapids, Mich.: W. B. Eerdmans, 1980).

6. James D. G. Dunn, *The Acts of the Apostles,* Epworth Commentaries (Peterborough: Epworth Press, 1996).

7. See Alfred Plummer, *A Critical and Exegetical Commentary on the Gospel According to St. Luke,* 5th ed., International Critical Commentary on the Holy Scriptures of the Old and New Testament (New York: C. Scribner's Sons, 1901) 564.

at Bethphage? Clearly Luke believed that all three places were closely associated, lying along the one road out of Jerusalem over the ridge of the Mount of Olives.

Therefore, my preference for the translation of Luke 24:50, doing justice to the Greek while not confusing the English reader, would be: "Then he led them out up to the point overlooking Bethany." Such a reading would be supported by the factors of geography and the need to retain the author's two descriptions, which are used for the different narrative purposes.

By clearing up such geographic confusions, I trust that we can refocus on the doctrine of the Ascension, so long neglected. The Ascension is the necessary completion of the Incarnation and the gateway to the exaltation of the Christ.

Reference Books

Atkins, Peter. *Worship 2000!* London: HarperCollins Religious, 1999.

Barrett, C. K. *A Critical and Exegetical Commentary on the Acts of the Apostles.* International Critical Commentary on the Holy Scriptures of the Old and New Testament 34. Edinburgh: T & T Clark, 1994.

Barth, Karl. *Prayer and Preaching.* London: SCM Press, 1964.

Benesch, Friedrich. *Ascension.* Edinburgh: Floris Books, 1979.

Buchanan, G. W. *The Epistle to the Hebrews.* Anchor Bible Series. New York: Doubleday, 1972.

Davies, J. G. *He Ascended into Heaven: A Study in the History of Doctrine.* London: Lutterworth Press, 1958.

Donne, Brian. *Christ Ascended.* Exeter: Paternoster Press, 1983.

Ellingworth, Paul. *The Epistle to the Hebrews.* London: Epworth Press, 1991.

_____. *The Epistle to the Hebrews: A Commentary on the Greek Text.* Grand Rapids, Mich.: Wm. B. Eerdmans/Carlisle: Paternoster Press, 1993.

Lane, William. *Hebrews 1–8.* Word Biblical Commentary 47. Dallas: Word Books, 1991.

Lindars, Barnabas. *The Theology of the Letter to the Hebrews.* Cambridge: Cambridge University Press, 1991.

Mackenzie, Iain. *The Dynamism of Space.* Norwich: The Canterbury Press, 1995.

Montefiore, H. W. *The Epistle to the Hebrews.* London: A & C Black, 1964.

Parsons, Mikeal C. *The Departure of Jesus in Luke-Acts.* Journal for the Study of the New Testament, Supplement Series 21. Sheffield: JSOT, Supplement, 1987.

Sampson, Fay. *Ascensiontide and Pentecost.* Exeter: Religious and Moral Education, 1986.

Stookey, L. H. *The Calendar: Christ's Time for the Church.* Nashville: Abingdon Press, 1996.

Torrance, T. F. *Space, Time and Resurrection.* Edinburgh: Handsel Press, 1976. Chapters 5–7.

Tutu, Desmond, and John Allen, eds. *The Rainbow People of God.* London: Doubleday, 1994.

Ward, Keith. *Religion and Creation.* Oxford: Oxford University Press, 1996.

Young, Francis, ed. *Dare We Speak of God in Public?* London and New York: Mowbray, 1995.

Index